Key stage 3

The Crusades

IAN DAWSON

Contents

Chapter one
Investigating the Crusades — 3

Chapter two
Christians and Moslems — 8

Chapter three
The victories of Saladin — 20

Chapter four
The most famous Crusade — 26

Chapter five
The Crusades: change and continuity — 34

Chapter six
What can we learn from the Crusades? — 40

Index — 48

Oxford University Press 1992

Oxford University Press,
Walton Street, Oxford OX2 6DP

Oxford New York Toronto
Delhi Bombay Calcutta Madras
Karachi Petaling Jaya Singapore
Hong Kong Tokyo Nairobi
Dar es Salaam Cape Town
Melbourne Auckland

and associated companies in
Berlin Ibadan

Oxford is a trademark of
Oxford University Press

© Oxford University Press 1992

ISBN 0 19 917 2102

Typeset by MS Filmsetting
Limited, Frome, Somerset
Printed in Hong Kong

Preface

Like the other books in this series The
Crusades is structured as an investigation. The
introduction establishes four questions and
invites pupils to suggest initial answers or
hypotheses, using the material in the
introduction and their existing ideas,
assumptions or prejudices. These first ideas
from groups or individuals should be recorded
(in pupils' books or as a wall-display) and then
developed as pupils explore each question in
more detail. A later comparison between the
initial answers and the final conclusions should
boost pupils' confidence by helping them
appreciate how much they have learned about
the Crusades and life in the Middle Ages.

The book has been designed to be used in its
own right or as a complement to a study of
Medieval Realms. Used in its own right, The
Crusades offers both depth and breadth of
coverage. Chapter 2 offers depth by examining
the different perspectives of people of the time
and Chapters 3 and 4 concentrate on the events
of the 1180's and 1190's, events and people that
pupils are most likely to have heard of.
Chapters 5 and 6 cover a much longer timespan,
investigating whether all Crusades were the
same and the consequences of the Crusades.

The Crusades can also be used to complement
Medieval Realms in this series. Medieval Realms
is an investigation into the degree of change in
the Middle Ages and The Crusades (particularly
Chapter 5) can be used as a case-study to test
the conclusions reached in Medieval Realms. If
using The Crusades as a case-study, teachers
may choose to investigate only some of the
questions in this book or divide the questions
amongst pupils, with different groups of pupils
working on each of the chapters.

Opportunities for recording pupils' work in
relation to Attainment Targets are provided in
the exercises indicated by the headings in the
chart on the right. Last but not least, I hope
that the material in The Crusades allows pupils
to understand that these events involved real
people, both famous and unknown, Moslems
and Christians who, like us, were sometimes
right and sometimes wrong, sometimes brave
and sometimes afraid, sometimes cruel and
sometimes kind.

Ian Dawson

Notes to teachers

Exercises offering opportunities for developing
pupils' understanding of concepts and skills
required in Attainment Targets are signposted
as follows. Most (but not all) of the questions in
these exercises are linked to Statements of
Attainment. Here and throughout the book
remorseless linking of questions to Attainment
Targets would have proved to be an intolerable
burden for everyone. However, questions at
the end of each chapter do open up
opportunities for explicit discussion of the
concepts that lie behind the Attainment
Targets. Such explicit discussion is vital for the
development of pupils' understanding.

AT1a Changes		Chapter 5 passim
AT1b Causes and		
	Consequences	25, 32, 46
AT1c People in the Past	15, 18, 19	
AT2 Different Views	40, 41, 42	
AT3 Evidence		11, 21, 23, 26, 28, 31, 33

Investigating the Crusades

One day, late in the autumn of 1095, thousands of people gathered in a field outside the town of Clermont in France. They were waiting for the Pope, Urban II. Everyone knew he was going to make an important speech. His words changed the lives of many, many people all over Europe and in the Middle East.

The Pope began by saying that he had terrible news from Jerusalem. The holy city had been captured by people 'completely foreign to God'. Churches had been destroyed and many people had been killed. Then the Pope asked the people:

'Who is to revenge all this, who is to repair this damage if you do not do it? Brave and valiant knights, remember the courage of your fathers. Do not let your love for your children, wives or parents hold you back. Remember that Jesus Christ said "Everyone who has left house or brothers or father or mother or wife or children or lands for my sake shall receive a hundred times more and life everlasting".

Our lands are too small for you. They do not have enough food or wealth for all of you. Because of this you fight each other. Stop these quarrels. Stop these wars. Begin the journey to Jerusalem. Win back that land which is richer than any other, a paradise of delights. This is the land where Jesus Christ lived and died. It longs for freedom. Take the journey and win glory in the Kingdom of Heaven.'

When Pope Urban finished, the people shouted, 'Deus Vult!' ('God wills it!'). Those words 'Deus Vult!' became the battle cry of the Crusaders – the people who wore the cross of Christ in their fight for Jerusalem. That speech began hundreds of years of Crusading wars.

Look back at Urban's speech. Why do you think some of the first Crusaders set out for Jerusalem?

Christian pilgrims had been visiting Jerusalem for centuries and had usually been welcomed by local Moslems.

✆ The Capture of Jerusalem

Pope Urban travelled to many other towns, asking more people to join the Crusade. He wanted soldiers — noblemen and knights — who would lead a strong and well-planned expedition. However, many poorer people were also excited by the idea of Crusade. Before the Pope's Crusade could begin, another Crusade, called the People's Crusade, began.

The leader of the People's Crusade was Peter the Hermit. Peter was an exciting speaker.

Thousands of people from France and Germany joined him. Men, women and children walked all the way to Constantinople but they were not a strong army. In October 1096 they were massacred by a Moslem army.

The Pope's Crusaders had only just started their journey. They planned their attack carefully and captured several important towns. They did not reach Jerusalem until June 1099. Then they surrounded the city and built wooden towers to help their attack. On 13 July, the final attack began.

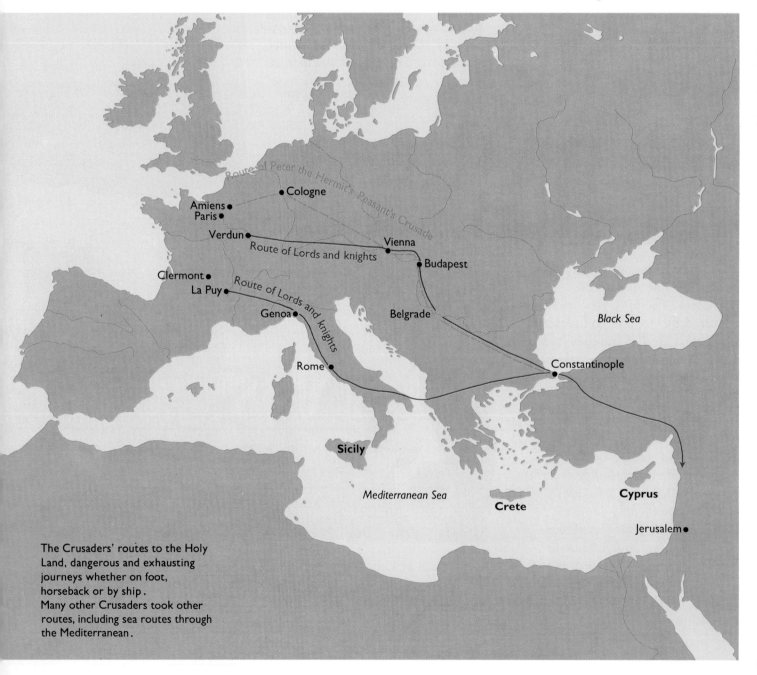

The Crusaders' routes to the Holy Land, dangerous and exhausting journeys whether on foot, horseback or by ship.
Many other Crusaders took other routes, including sea routes through the Mediterranean.

Source A

Before we attacked the city, the bishops ordered everyone to hold a procession in honour of God all round the city and arranged for prayers. At dawn we attacked the city from all sides, without making any headway. We were all trembling and stunned. Then Duke Godfrey and his brother made a fierce attack. One of our knights, called Lethold, climbed over the city wall. All the city's defenders fled from the wall. Our men followed, killing and beheading them all the way to the Temple of Solomon. There was such a slaughter for a whole day but, finally, they were beaten. Our men captured men and women. They killed them or let them live as they saw fit. Soon our men were running all round the city, seizing gold and silver, horses and mules and houses filled with all kinds of goods.

(From a chronicle called *The Deeds of the Franks*, written by a soldier who went on the Crusade)

The Crusaders chose Duke Godfrey of Bouillon as King of Jerusalem. They kept control of Jerusalem for 88 years but then a Moslem army recaptured the city. Source B is a Moslem account of the capture of Jerusalem in 1187.

Source B

When the Franks saw how violently the Moslems were attacking, they became desperate. They decided to ask for safe-conduct out of Jerusalem and to hand the city over to Saladin. Saladin refused their request. 'We shall deal with you', he said, 'just as you dealt with the people of Jerusalem when you took it with murder, slavery and other savageries'. Then Lord Balian said 'if we see that death is inevitable, then by God we shall kill our children and our wives, burn our possessions so as not to leave you anything. We shall pull down your sacred places and kill all the Moslem prisoners we have – 5000 of them. Then we shall come out fighting and die with honour or win a noble victory!'

Then Saladin and his advisers agreed to give the Franks promises of safety if each man paid ten dinar, children two and women five dinar. All who paid this should go free. The others would be slaves. Lord Balian gave 30,000 dinar to ransom the poor. Saladin set the Queen of Jerusalem free and let her take her belongings and servants. The Archbishop of Jerusalem took great treasures and money. Saladin was advised to seize these treasures but he said he would not go back on his word.

(From *The Sum of World History* by Ibn al-Athir, who lived 1160–1233)

The Holy Sepulchre
The Christian church built on the site of Calvary (where Christ was crucified) and of the tomb of Christ.

The Dome of the Rock
The centre of Moslem pilgrimages to Jerusalem. It was the site of Muhammad's ascent to heaven.

THE BEGINNING OF THE CRUSADES

1 Why do you think people went on Crusades?
2 Why was Jerusalem important to Moslems?
3 Was religion important to people in the Middle Ages? Explain your answer.
4 Do you think the Christians and Moslems admired or hated each other? Explain your answer.

When were the Crusades?

The Crusades began when Pope Urban made the speech at Clermont in 1095. They did not end when Saladin re-captured Jerusalem in 1187.

The timeline below will help you understand when the Crusades happened.

Crusades in Europe against people who disagreed with the Catholic religion

Crusades against non-Christians in Eastern Europe

Crusades to the Holy Land   Preaching and planning of Crusades to the Holy Land

Crusades to Spain against the Moslem Moors

1099 Crusaders capture Jerusalem

1187 Moslems recapture Jerusalem

● Major Crusades

Western soldiers used the same equipment as they did in Europe – heavy chain mail and armour and horses bred for massed charges. Moslem soldiers were much more lightly armoured with smaller, faster horses for raiding.

WHEN WERE THE CRUSADES?

1 How long did the Crusades last?
2 When was fighting most common?
3 Did all the Crusades aim to capture Jerusalem?
4 When were the Crusaders most successful?
5 When were the Moslems most successful?
6 Which event or events do you think were the most important turning points in the history of the Crusades?

Investigating the Crusades

The Crusades were wars between Christians and non-Christians. The most famous Crusades were against Moslem armies to capture Jerusalem, the holy city.

This book will help you to investigate some important questions about the Crusades. Chapter 2 will investigate why the two groups – Christian and Moslem – could not live together peacefully. Chapters 3 and 4 will investigate why the Moslem armies recaptured and kept control of Jerusalem after 1187. Chapters 5 and 6 will investigate whether all Crusades were the same and the consequences of the Crusades.

You may already have some ideas about an answer to the first of these questions. You can find clues on this page and on pages 3–6. To start your investigation look again at these pages and then write down your first answer to this question.

Historians call this first answer a hypothesis. As you work through this book you will be able to form, check and improve your four hypotheses. The chart below shows you this process. Is this the same way you study other subjects, such as science?

Start with questions	Suggest your first ideas or hypotheses	Investigate your evidence	Improve your first hypothesis
Why couldn't they live together peacefully?	Possible Answers: different religions and language. Past cruelties?	**More evidence** pages 8–19	?
Why did the Moslems win control of Jerusalem?	Possible Answers: Better leaders and soldiers. Crusaders far from home.	**More evidence** pages 20–33	?
Were all the Crusades the same? What were the consequences of the Crusades?	?	**More evidence** pages 34–47	?

The greatest of the Crusader castles, Krak des Chevaliers (Castle of the Knights), was built in the late twelfth century

Christians and Moslems

In 1100 the Crusaders controlled Jerusalem and some other small areas. However, these areas were wide apart and there was great danger of losing them if the Moslems counter-attacked. Therefore, the Crusaders fought to win more land until their lands were all part of one connected kingdom.

Even then, the Crusaders still only had a thin strip of land, surrounded by huge areas controlled by Moslems. It looked as if the Crusaders could be crushed easily, but the Moslems were not united. Different groups of Moslems were more interested in fighting each other than fighting the Franks, as they called the Christians. One powerful group, the Fatimids, were based in Egypt. The other was the Seljuk Turks, who had an Empire north-east of the Crusader kingdoms. Before the first Crusaders arrived, these groups had been fighting each other for control of Jerusalem. These fights between Moslems made the Crusaders' task much easier.

County of Edessa

Principality of Antioch

County of Tripoli

Moslem lands

Kingdom of Jerusalem

- Edessa
- Antioch
- Tripoli
- Beirut
- Tyre
- Acre
- Jaffa
- Jerusalem

☐ 1098–1100
☐ 1100–1144

This map shows the extent of the Crusader conquests up to 1144

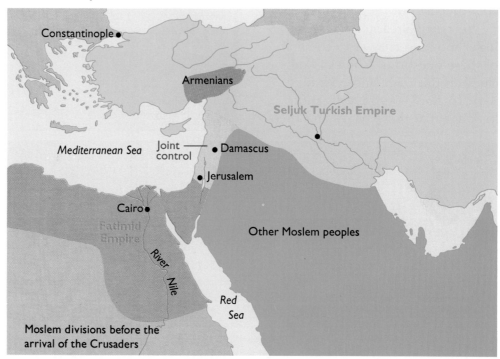

Moslem divisions before the arrival of the Crusaders

Constantinople

Armenians

Seljuk Turkish Empire

Mediterranean Sea

Joint control — Damascus

Jerusalem

Cairo

Fatimid Empire

River Nile

Red Sea

Other Moslem peoples

Christians from Europe were not the only people living in the Crusader lands. The newcomers filled the towns and the castles but the local people — some Moslems and some Christians — lived in the villages and on the farms. It is easy to think that the Crusaders brought Christianity back to the region, but there had been Christians in the Holy Land since the time of Christ. Therefore, the different peoples had to live side by side. They bought and sold food and other goods from each other. Moslem villagers had Christian lords and paid taxes to them. Most of them lived together in peace — but war was never far away.

This chapter will help you investigate why war was almost certain to continue between Christian and Moslem armies. What ideas do you already have for an answer to this question?

Why couldn't they live together peacefully?

※ We used to be Westerners

Many Crusaders stayed and settled in the Kingdom of Jerusalem. Many of them changed the way they lived to fit the climate. Many also picked up new ideas from the Moslems they met. They began to use glass in their windows and mosaic tiles on their floors. They had many more baths, used soap, and even wore long cotton robes, which were much more comfortable in the hot weather. Some settlers also began to use Arab doctors and medicines. Look at the information on this page and then answer the questions below.

Source A

The Christians make the Moslem traders pay a tax which is collected fairly. The Christian traders also pay a tax on their goods to the Moslems when they travel through the Moslems' lands. The two sides understand each other completely. The men of war fight their war but the people stay at peace.

(Ibn Jubayr, 1144–1217. He was a Moslem trader from Spain who travelled through the Middle East in 1182–1185)

Source B

We travelled through many farms and villages whose lands are well farmed. The people are all Moslems but they live in comfort with the Franks – may God preserve us from temptation! Their houses belong to them and their property is unharmed. All the land, villages and farms stayed in the hands of the Moslems.

(Ibn Jubayr, 1144–1217)

Source C

We used to be Westerners, now we are Easterners. The men who were from Rome or France have become Galileans or Palestinians. We have already forgotten the places where we were born. Some have married women from this land, either Christians or Moslems who have been baptised.

(Fulcher of Chartres, 1059–1127. He joined the First Crusade in 1096 and lived in Jerusalem until he died. He wrote a detailed history of the Crusaders)

Source D

Our princes, because of the influence of their women, scorn the medicine of our European doctors and believe only in Jews, Syrians and Moslems. Foolishly, they put themselves in the care of such people and trust their lives to people who are ignorant of medicine.

(William of Tyre, 1130–1185. He spent most of his life in the Kingdom of Jerusalem and became Archbishop of Tyre. He wrote a history of the Kings of Jerusalem)

Sometimes individuals became friends despite the wars. This picture shows a Christian and Moslem playing chess.

Many of the Crusaders came from castles looking like this. Everyone ate and most people slept in the Great Hall.

CRUSADERS IN THE EAST

1 What evidence is there of Crusaders changing the way they lived?
2 What evidence is there of Christians and Moslems getting on well together?
3 Which source is the best evidence of friendship between Christians and Moslems? Give reasons for your answer.
4 What do you think new Crusaders arriving from Europe thought about the way the Christian settlers lived?

✳ The Stories of Usamah

The most famous writer about the way Moslems and Christians lived together was Usamah Ibn Munqidh. Usamah was born in 1095, the year that Urban preached the First Crusade, and died in 1188, shortly after the Moslems recaptured Jerusalem. Usamah was a rich Moslem nobleman. He knew all the Moslem leaders and many of the Crusaders' leaders. He travelled widely from his castle at Shaizar, near Antioch. You can find Shaizar on the map on page 13.

When he was old, Usamah wrote the story of his life. It is full of his adventures in wars and out hunting. He also wrote about the people he met, including the Crusaders or 'the Franks'. Like other Moslems, Usamah called all the Crusaders 'Franks', whether they came from France, England, Italy or any other country. Here are some of his stories.

The interior of an Arab castle
Usamah lived in conditions like this. Compare this with the western castle on page 9.

Source E

We notice the Franks who have become used to living among Moslems. They are greatly superior to the Franks who have only recently come to this country. They are, however, the exception that must not become the rule.

I sent one of my friends to Antioch on business. One day the chief of the city said to my friend, 'I have received an invitation from one of my Frankish friends; come with me and see their customs'.

This is what my friend told me. 'We entered the house of one of the old knights who came on the first Frankish expedition. He was no longer a soldier. Servants brought in a magnificent table furnished with the most perfect food. However, my host noticed that I was not eating. "Eat" he said to me, "you will find it good. For I too do not eat Frankish food, but I have Egyptian cooks and I only eat what they cook. No pork ever comes into my house". I decided to eat, but with care.

Some days later I was in the market-place when a Frankish woman shouted at me in their barbarous language. I did not understand a word. A crowd gathered round me. They were Franks and I began to feel that my death was close. Then the old knight appeared. "What do you want with this Moslem?" he said to the woman. "He is the soldier who killed my brother", she said. "No", said the Christian knight, "he is a merchant, who does not fight in battles." The crowd went away. He took my hand and went with me. Thanks to that meal I escaped certain death'.

Source F

Glory be to Allah, the creator and author of all things! Anyone who knows the Franks can only praise Allah the All-Powerful for he has seen in them animals who are greater in courage and in enthusiasm for fighting but in nothing else, just as animals are superior in strength and aggression.

There was a good Frankish knight who had come to make a pilgrimage and then go home. We became so friendly that he called me 'my brother'. We liked each other and often spent time together. When he was ready to go home he said to me, 'My brother, I am returning home and I would like, with your permission, to take your son to see my countries (my son was 14). He will see our knights and he will learn wisdom. When he returns he will be an intelligent man.' I was hurt by his words, which did not come from a wise head. Being taken prisoner would have been better than going to the Frankish countries. I answered, 'By your life, I hoped he could go with you but his grandmother made me promise that I would not let him go.'

Source G

The Franks who have come recently are always more inhuman than the Franks who have lived long among us and are used to Moslems.

A proof of the harshness of the Franks (the scourge of Allah upon them!) can be seen in what happened to me when I visited Jerusalem. I went into the mosque Al-Aqsa. By the side was a little mosque that the Franks had made into a church. The Christian Templars were in charge of the mosques. They were my friends and let me say my prayers in the little mosque. I was praying when a Frank rushed at me, seized me and turned my face to the East, saying 'That is how to pray!' A group of Templars took hold of him and threw him out. I returned to my prayers. The same Frank came back and forced my face around to the East, repeating 'That is how to pray!' The Templars again threw him out and they apologised to me. 'He is a stranger who has only just arrived. He has never seen anyone praying without turning to the east.' I went out and saw how he was trembling with shock after seeing me pray towards Mecca.

Source H

The Franks (may Allah turn from them!) have none of the virtues of men except bravery. The knights are really the only important men among them. At that time there was peace between us. I said to King Fulk, 'Lord Renier stole my sheep at lambing time. The lambs died at birth. He gave the sheep back after the lambs died.' The King said to six or seven knights, 'Decide what would be fair.' They left the room and discussed the problem. Then they returned and said, 'Lord Renier should pay for the loss of the lambs.' The king ordered him to pay and I finally accepted 400 dinars from him. Once the knights have made a decision no-one can alter it.

The Knights Templars and Hospitallers were monks as well as knights. Their castles were also monasteries. They had vowed to fight for Christianity and Jerusalem and they were the greatest and most unforgiving opponents of the Moslem forces. This is a Templar from the fourteenth century.

EVIDENCE: THE STORIES OF USAMAH

1 a In Source E how can you tell the old knight was used to living with Moslems?
   b What evidence is there that many Christians did not agree with the old knight?

2 a In Source F what did Usamah admire about the Franks?
   b Why did Usamah say that he had promised to take the boy home to his grandmother?

3 a In Source G why did the Frankish knight grab hold of Usamah?
   b Why did the Templars treat him differently?

4 In Source H did Usamah think the Franks treated him fairly?
   Now use all the stories.

5 Did Usamah like or hate the Franks? Explain your answer.

6 Do you think that Usamah wanted the Franks to stay or did he want them driven out? Explain your answer.

7 Are Usamah's stories useful evidence for investigating the way Moslems and Christians lived together? Explain your answer.

8 How do Usamah's stories help to explain why fighting did not stop?

✵ Moslem ideas and fears

The evidence you have seen so far says that some Moslems and Christians lived together peacefully. However, Usamah's comments suggest that they were never completely happy. After he mentions a Frank he usually adds words like 'the curse of Allah upon him'. In the first story he said that he did not want the peaceful Franks 'to become the rule'. So even though individuals could become friends, peace between the two groups was not likely to last long. Now we need to look at each group – Moslems and Christians – to see why they could not live together peacefully for long. The diagram on the left shows four reasons why Moslems could not live peacefully with Christians. Copy the diagram and then look at the sources on this page and on pages 13–15. Which sources give evidence to support each of the four reasons? Fill in the source letters in the correct places on your copy of the diagram.

Religion was at the centre of everyday life and was different from the Christian religion

Sources …

Fear of being conquered and horror at the actions of some Crusaders

Sources …

Why didn't the Moslems live peacefully with the Christians?

Differences in attitudes and the way they lived

Sources …

Leaders united the Moslems and wanted to fight back

Sources …

Source A

Jerusalem was a Holy City to the Moslems because it was the site of Muhammad's ascension to heaven. Most Christians did not understand the importance of this. This Moslem picture shows Muhammad ascending to heaven.

Source B

Imad al-Din Zangi was a handsome man, more than 60 years old when he died. His people and his army went in fear of him. Under his government the strong dared not harm the weak. Before he came to power the lack of strong rulers and the presence of the Franks had made the country a wilderness but he made it flower again.

(Ibn Al Athir, 1160–1233. He was a historian whose main work was *A Perfect History*, which filled 13 books. Zangi recaptured Edessa from the Crusaders in 1144 but was murdered two years later. He also had to fight other Moslem leaders, who allied with the Crusaders to stop Zangi gaining more power)

Source C

The governor of Al-Mounaitira asked my uncle to send a doctor to look after some urgent cases. My uncle chose a Christian doctor called Thabit who was away only 10 days. He said 'they brought to me a knight with an abscess on his leg and a woman sick with fever. I applied a little ointment to the knight and his abscess improved. I fed the woman certain food and she improved.

Then a Frankish doctor came up and said "this man cannot cure them!" He said to the knight, "do you want to live with one leg or die with two?" The knight answered, "I would rather live with one leg". The Frankish doctor stretched the leg on a wooden block and said to another knight, "cut off his leg with the hatchet in one blow". Before my eyes this man aimed two blows and the knight died instantly.

As for the woman, the doctor said, "there is a devil who has possessed her. Shave off her hair." This was done and she returned to her old diet. Her fever became worse. The doctor said, "The devil has entered her head." Taking a razor he cut open her head in the shape of a cross and scraped away the skin so that the bone was showing. He rubbed salt into her head. The woman died.'

(Usamah Ibn Munqidh, 1095–1188)

Source D

Forty ship loads of Frankish soldiers arrived at Beirut to assault the city on Friday 13 May 1110. They brought up two siege-towers and fought ferociously. In the end the defenders lost heart, seeing no escape from certain death. The governor fled with a few companions but they were brought back by the Franks and executed. The city was ransacked, the people captured and enslaved, and their money and belongings stolen. The people of Sidon feared a fate like that of Beirut. They asked Baldwin to spare their lives and, reassured by his promise, the governor, the soldiers and many of the people left and went to Damascus. Baldwin taxed the remaining Moslems to their last penny, reducing them to poverty. He used force to get money from people who were hiding it.

(Ibn al Qalanisi, 1073–1160. He was an important official in Damascus who wrote a history using eye-witness accounts and his own experiences as sources)

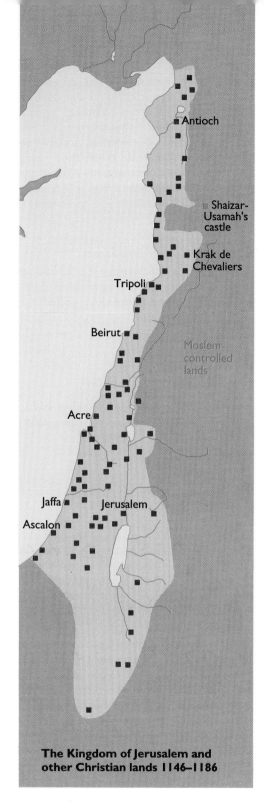

The Kingdom of Jerusalem and other Christian lands 1146–1186

Source E

The Crusaders built castles all over the Holy Land. They were homes for the lords of the Kingdom of Jerusalem and they were also vital defences. Each red square shows the position of a Crusader castle.

Source F

i At Ma'arra scraps of flesh from the pagans' bodies were discovered. When starvation forced our soldiers to the deed of cannibalism a hideous rumour spread amongst the pagans – that there were men in the Christian army who fed greedily on the bodies of Moslems. When they heard this some of the Christian army roasted the body of a Moslem over a fire as if it were meat for eating, in full view of their army.

(Abbot Guibert of Nogent, 1064–1125. He wrote a history of the First Crusade although he did not travel to the Holy Land)

ii In Ma'arra our troops boiled pagan adults in cooking pots; they impaled children on spits and devoured them grilled.

(Radulph of Caen, who travelled to the Holy Land in the early 1100's and wrote a chronicle of the Crusades)

Source G

The five pillars of Islam

All Moslems share these beliefs and ideals.

Giving alms
Moslems must give 2½% of their wealth to charity for the poor.

Prayer
Moslems must pray five times each day. They must cleanse themselves in running water before prayer.

Belief
There is only one God, Allah. Muhammad is his most important prophet.

Fasting
Moslems must fast from dawn to dusk during the month of Ramadan. It is a time to think about past sins and to show concern for the poor.

Pilgrimages
Moslems are expected to make a pilgrimage to Mecca at least once in their lifetime. Other holy cities are Medina and Jerusalem.

Source H

There is no excuse before God for a Moslem to stay in a city of unbelief, unless he is merely passing through. In the land of Islam he finds shelter from the discomfort and evils he meets in the countries of the Christians, where he hears disgusting words spoken about the Prophet, finds it impossible to cleanse himself or has to live among pigs. One of the horrors of Christian countries is the sight of Moslem prisoners tottering in chains, treated as slaves.

(Ibn Jubayr, 1144–1217. A Moslem trader from Spain, he was horrified to see Moslems living at peace amongst the Crusaders in the Holy Land)

Source I

The Al-Aqsa mosque was a den of pigs and filth, crammed full with new buildings of theirs, occupied by all kinds of evil-doers and criminals. It would have been a crime to delay in purifying it.

(From the writings of Imad ad-Din, who was secretary to Saladin. He is describing the state of the holiest Moslem shrine in Jerusalem when the Moslems recaptured it in 1187)

Source J

Nur ad-Din's kingdom extended far and wide and his power was acknowledged even in Medina, Mecca and the Yemen. He was known throughout his realms as a wise and just ruler. He had a good knowledge of Moslem law and would not permit the collection of illegal taxes in any of his lands in Egypt, Syria, the Sazira and Mosul. On the battlefield he had no equal.

(Ibn al-Athir writing about the Moslems' leader, Nur ad-Din, the son of Zangi, who died in 1174)

Source K

Reports came of the coming of the king of the Franks with so many soldiers they could not be counted. They were said to be making for the land of Islam, having sent orders throughout their lands for people to leave their homes and set out on the expedition. Some said there were more than a million on horseback and on foot. Others said there were even more.

(Ibn al Qalanisi)

Source L

Among the Frankish prisoners was an old woman with a son and a daughter. The son, Raoul, became a Moslem and took his prayers and fasting seriously. He learnt to work in marble and paved my father's house in marble. My father married him to a Moslem woman of good family and gave him everything necessary for his house. His wife bore him two sons who were five or six years old when their father took them, his wife and all their possessions to rejoin the Franks. He became Christian again, together with his children, after many years of Moslem faith and prayer. May Allah the Most High cleanse the world of this race.

(Usamah Ibn Munqidh)

Source M

The way of life in the east was very different from that in Europe. Moslems thought the western way of life was very strange and, therefore, wrong. They could not imagine living at peace with people who were so different from themselves.

PEOPLE IN THE PAST: MOSLEM ATTITUDES TO THE CRUSADERS

1 Look at your completed diagram. The four reasons were not really separate but were linked together.
   a How might religion and Moslem fears of the Crusaders help Moslem leaders to fight back?
   b How were Moslem fears and their different way of life linked to their religion?

2 Do you think that all Moslems had the same attitudes to the Crusaders?
3 Most Moslems, like Usamah, cursed the Franks with words like: 'The curse of Allah be upon them.' Why did they curse the Franks?
4 Look back to your first hypothesis. Do you want to add or change anything after working on this section?

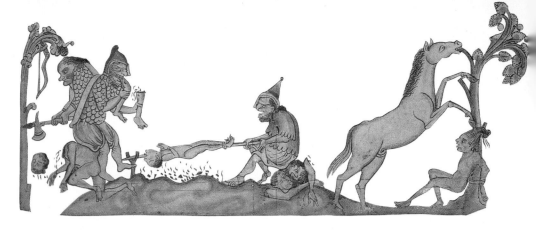

Source N

Horror stories about cannibalism were told by both sides. This scene is a Christian picture, showing Moslems roasting their victims.

✤ The Crusaders' ideas and fears

Now you have a good idea why the Moslems could not live without fear of the Crusaders. The Crusaders were just as worried about the Moslems, even though there were periods of peace. Pages 16–18 will help you to discover why the Crusaders could not live at peace for long with the Moslems.

Source O

The lands won back and unified by the Moslem leaders, Zangi and Nur ad-Din

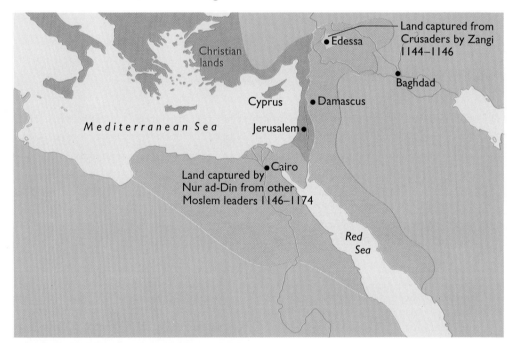

Land captured from Crusaders by Zangi 1144–1146

Christian lands

• Edessa

• Baghdad

Cyprus

• Damascus

Jerusalem •

Mediterranean Sea

• Cairo

Land captured by Nur ad-Din from other Moslem leaders 1146–1174

Red Sea

Source P

Soldiers who were captured were usually ransomed or sold as slaves. However, both sides sometimes executed prisoners in revenge. This picture shows Christians awaiting execution by their Moslem captors.

Source Q

Sir, I am very sorry for you and for the country; for you will only be king and keep the country as long as the Moslems wish. There are Moslems living in all the towns of your country. If a Moslem army entered your country it would have food, help and information from the peasants of the land. If the Moslems were beaten they would be helped to safety. If you were beaten your peasants would do you the most harm.

(From the Chronicle of Ernoul, written around 1260. These are the imaginary words of King Thoros of Armenia to King Amaury of Jerusalem in about 1165) ·

The destruction of the Holy Sepulchre by Moslem forces in 1009 was remembered by Christians, even though later Moslem rulers had allowed pilgrims to visit Jerusalem freely

Source R

King Baldwin of Jerusalem obtained certain pills from Barac, the doctor of the court, to keep off winter illnesses. Our princes in the Holy Land, through the influence of their women, scorn the medicine of our western doctors and believe only in the Jews, Syrians and Saracens.

Recklessly they trust their lives to such people who are ignorant of the science of medicine. It was rumoured that these pills were poisoned and this was probably a fact. When some of the medicine was given to a dog the animal died. As soon as the King took the first pills he became ill.

(William of Tyre, 1130–1183. He spent most of his life in the Holy Land. Compare this view of Moslem medicine with Usamah's view of western doctors in source C on page 13)

Source S

The Franks have no sense of honour. If one of them is walking in the street with his wife and meets another man, that man will take his wife's hand and draw her aside and speak to her, while the husband stands waiting for them to finish their conversation. If it lasts too long, the husband may leave her and go off!

(Usamah Ibn Munqidh)

Source U

We have forgotten the place where we were born. We new arrivals have become residents. Those who were needy have been enriched by God. Those who had a few pennies, here possess countless bezants. He who did not have a village, here has a God-given city. Why should anyone who has found the East return to the West (Europe)? God does not wish those who have taken the cross to be poor.

(Fulcher of Chartres, 1059–1127). He joined the First Crusade and lived in Jerusalem until he died)

This picture shows that each Crusader was a mixture of soldier and religious pilgrim

Source T

New Crusaders constantly arrived from Europe. They did not understand the attitude of settlers like Fulcher of Chartres who wrote that 'The lion and ox shall eat straw side by side. He who was a foreigner is now just like a native'.

Source V

This map of the world shows the importance of their religion to Christians. It was drawn with Jerusalem in the centre of the world.

Source W

Another shocking deed of this cruel enemy was that they pulled down with ropes the cross on the church of the Hospital. They smashed the cross and spat on it, then dragged it through the city dungheap as an insult to our religion.'

(From *The Journey of King Richard*, written in the early 1200's by an English churchman. It was based on eyewitness accounts. This describes what happened after the Moslems captured Jerusalem in 1187)

Source X

Go forward in safety, knights, and drive off the enemies of the cross of Christ. Neither death nor life can separate you from the love of God which is in Jesus Christ. How glorious are the victors who return from battle! How blessed are the martyrs who died in battle! Rejoice if you live and conquer in the Lord, but rejoice and glory more if you die and go to join the Lord.

(St Bernard of Clairvaux's words to the Knights Templar. These soldier–priests were dedicated to fighting for their religion)

Source Y

Twelve of us went to the church of St Peter with Peter Bartholomew who had told how God had sent him messages about the Holy Lance. We dug from morning to evening until some began to think we would never find the lance. When Bartholomew saw we were tiring he implored us to pray to God to give us the lance and so help us to victory. At last God showed us the lance. I cannot say how much joy filled the city.

(From Raymond of Aguilers' chronicle of the First Crusade. Raymond was a priest who went on the Crusade. Here he describes the finding of the Holy Lance which pierced Christ's side during the Crucifixion. Other writers told a different story. Radulph of Caen said that Bartholomew's discovery was an old Arab spear that he hid under his clothing and then put in the hole while no-one was looking)

PEOPLE IN THE PAST: THE CRUSADERS' ATTITUDES TO THE MOSLEMS

1 Look at sources N to Q. What reasons can you find for the Crusaders' fear of Moslem attacks?
2 Look at sources R to T. What do they tell you about the different attitudes and ideas of Christians and Moslems?
3 Why would the people described in source U be determined to fight back against the Moslems?
4 Look at sources V to Y. What reason do they give for war between the two groups?
5 Draw your own diagram like the one on page 12, showing why the Crusaders could not live in peace with the Moslems.
6 Look at your hypothesis. Make any final additions or changes-so you have a full answer to the question 'Why couldn't they live together in peace?'

✳ Understanding People in the Past

In this chapter you have been investigating why the Moslems and Christians could not live peacefully together. The diagram below shows you the reasons for their fear, distrust and hatred of each other. Do you think they really understood much about each other?

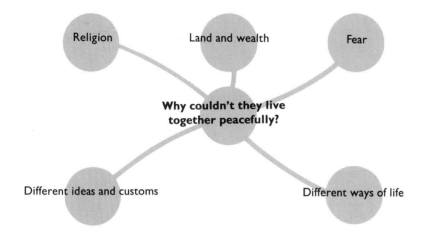

You have not just been learning about Moslems and Christians long ago. You have also been learning more about how we study history and answer questions about the past. In this chapter we have been answering a question about why something – war – happened. When we try to answer questions like this, which try to explain why things happened, we need to understand the ideas and feelings of the people at the time. Here are four things you may have discovered about the ideas and feelings of people in the past. Can you think of examples of them from this chapter?

In an historical investigation we need to discover:	Clues	Your examples
What people's ideas and attitudes were in the past	Christians and Moslems together	?
Whether everyone had the same ideas and attitudes at the time	new Crusaders and old settlers	?
Why they had those ideas and attitudes	swords and Bibles, scimitars and the Koran	?
Whether an individual's ideas and attitudes were complicated	Usamah	?

The victories of Saladin

One of the main reasons why the first Crusaders captured Jerusalem was that the Moslems were fighting amongst themselves. They did not join together to fight the Crusaders until it was too late. You can see a map of the different Moslem groups on page 8.

The first Moslem leader to fight back successfully was Imad al-Din Zangi. Zangi recaptured the city of Edessa and lands in the north of the Holy Land in 1144. However, the Moslems were still not united behind him and Zangi was murdered by Moslem enemies in 1146.

The lands regained by Zangi and Nur ad-Din.

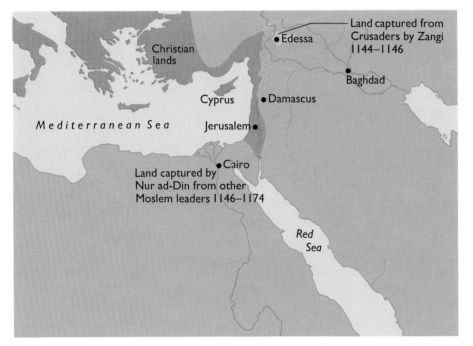

The lands regained by Saladin

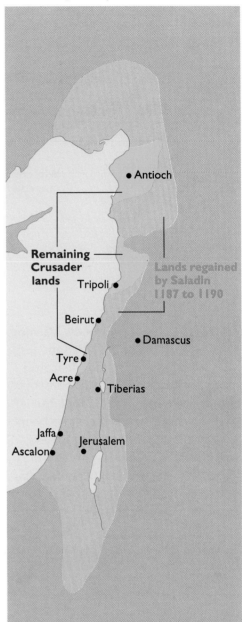

Zangi's son, Nur ad-Din, continued his father's fight and was even more successful. He won control of the important city of Damascus and of Egypt. By 1174 he had united the Moslems and completely surrounded the Crusader kingdom of Jerusalem. Nur ad-Din's death in 1174 could have helped the Crusaders but one of his generals, Saladin, stopped the Moslems splitting apart again. If

you look at the map above you can see that Saladin reconquered large areas of the Crusader kingdom. His greatest victory was the Battle of Hattin in July 1187. A few months later he recaptured Jerusalem. In this chapter you will be investigating this famous leader, Saladin, and his successes.

≋ *Why was Saladin successful?*

◁◑ Saladin

At first Saladin had to struggle to win the support of other Moslems. People said he was an upstart who had no right to be the new leader. Gradually, sometimes by war, sometimes through friendship, he won control over the Moslem lands. What was Saladin like?

Source A

Saladin was very generous. No one ever had to turn to others for help. It is impossible to count or detail all the gifts he gave. He was one of the most courageous of men. On the day of the great battle on the plain of Acre the centre of the Moslem army broke, drums and flags fell to the ground but he stood firm before leading his men back into battle, shaming them into turning and fighting.

(From Baha ad-Din's biography of Saladin. Baha ad-Din was a member of Saladin's household from 1188 to 1193)

Source B

From the time he began the holy war he did not spend one gold or silver coin except on the holy war or religious works. He was well-mannered and entertaining. He could recite by heart the histories of the Arab tribes. He had studied the wonders and curiosities of the world. Those who sat with him learned things they would never have heard elsewhere. If anyone was sick he would ask after him. He always kept his promise. I never heard him insult anyone or allow others to do so.

(From Baha ad-Din's biography of Saladin)

Source C

He was a wise man, valiant in war and generous beyond all measure.

(William of Tyre, 1130–1185. He spent most of his life in the kingdom of Jerusalem and became Archbishop of Tyre)

Source D

Saladin sent men out of Jerusalem to greet the Bishop of Salisbury and his party of pilgrims and show them to the holy places. He asked the bishop to stay in his palace, entertained him at his own expense and sent him many gifts.

(From *The Journey of King Richard*, written by an English churchman in the early 1200's. It was based on eye-witness accounts)

Source F

Saladin was never really firm in his decisions. If the defenders of a city resisted him for some time he would give up and abandon the siege. The best example of this was at Tyre. It was his fault alone that the Moslems suffered a setback before the walls of that city.

(Ibn al Athir, 1160–1233, a Moslem historian)

Source G

One of our soldiers deserted to the enemy. Saladin said 'Bring me the man who was next to the deserter.' They went and brought him. Saladin said 'Take him away to be killed'.

(Usamah ibn Munquidh, 1095–1188, a Moslem landowner)

Source H

Saladin sent gifts and messages to King Richard, gaining time by false and clever words. He kept none of his promises.

(From *The Journey of King Richard*, written in the early 1200's)

Source E

A western picture of Saladin, drawn in England. The artist optimistically shows Saladin being defeated by Richard I.

Source I

This is the only Moslem picture of Saladin. There are very few descriptions either, but we know he was surprisingly short and frail. His full name was Salah ad-Din Yusuf Ibn Ayyub. He died in 1193.

EVIDENCE: SALADIN

1 Read Sources A and B. Did Baha ad-Din admire Saladin?
2 Read Sources A–D. Why did people admire Saladin?
3 Read Source F. What does it criticise Saladin for?
4 Read Sources G and H.
   a How could you use these sources to praise Saladin?
   b How could you use these sources to criticise Saladin?
5 Which source gives the best evidence for **a** Saladin's generosity and **b** Saladin's cleverness?
6 Do the pictures (Sources E and I) give us any valuable evidence about **a** Saladin and **b** anything else?
7 Write your own description of Saladin using the information and sources on pages 20–21.

The Battle of Hattin

Saladin's most important victory was the Battle of Hattin in 1187. Late in June he crossed the River Jordan into the heart of the Kingdom of Jerusalem with an army of 30,000 men, including 12,000 well-trained cavalry. King Guy of Jerusalem had the largest Christian army ever raised in the Holy Land but it was still outnumbered. He had 20,000 men, including 1,200 knights.

The Crusaders camped at Sephorie where they had a good water supply and defences. Saladin was determined to fight a battle quickly so he sent part of his army to attack the town of Tiberias. This gave the Crusaders a serious problem.

The movements of the armies before the battle.

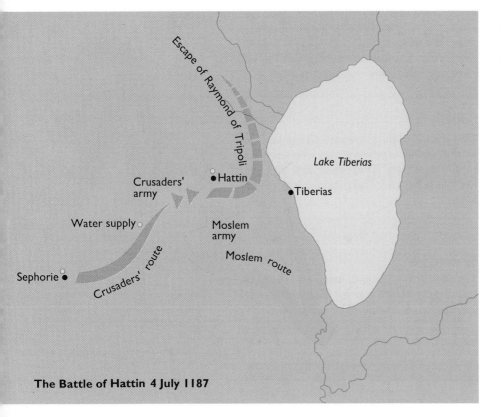

The Battle of Hattin 4 July 1187

Source J

When the Franks heard that Saladin had won the town of Tiberias they met in council. Some wanted to march against the Moslems to stop them taking the castle at Tiberias. Lord Raymond interrupted, saying 'Tiberias belongs to me. My wife is besieged in the castle but I would let the castle and my wife be captured if I could be sure Saladin's attack would stop there. I have never seen a Moslem army so large or so powerful. We must avoid a battle. We can always recapture Tiberias and ransom the prisoners later.' But Reynold of Châtillon said, 'You are trying to frighten us with your talk of the Moslem army because you are friendly with them. As for the size of their army, a large load of fuel will be good for the fires of hell.'

(Ibn al Athir, 1160–1233. A Moslem historian)

King Guy decided to march to the rescue of Tiberias. Soon his army began to suffer badly from the great heat. They had little water. When they turned north in search of water they were surrounded by Saladin's army on the Horns of Hattin. Sources K and L give us two accounts of the battle.

Source K

To cut a long story short, so many were killed, so many wounded and so many thrown into chains that our army was completely destroyed. Worse still, the Holy Cross was taken by the enemy. When King Guy saw the Cross fall he rushed forward and flung his arms round it, hoping to snatch it back, if God so willed, or die beside it. So the Holy Cross suffered another insult because of our wickedness.

When the noise of battle ended, Saladin raised his eyes to heaven and thanked God for his victory as he always did when things went well for him. He frequently said that our sins, not his power, gave him this victory.

(From *The Journey of King Richard*, written in the early 1200's by an English churchman. It was based on eye-witness accounts)

Source L

Our army stood between the Franks and Lake Tiberias. Devastated by thirst they stood patiently. Then, desperately, they drank whatever water they had. They camped bewildered, drunk with thirst, yearning for the lake. The Sultan Saladin moved among his soldiers, encouraging them and promising them the victory they expected from God. Our army was strengthened by the sight of him. They blocked the enemy's attack and threw them back. Some of our holy warriors set fire to the grass. Its flames bore down on the enemy and the heat became intense. The Franks suffered the fire of flames, the fire of thirst and the fire of arrows.

No matter how hard they fought they were beaten back. They retreated to Mount Hattin but they were surrounded. God gave the victory to the Sultan Saladin.

(Imad ad-Din, Saladin's secretary and chronicler)

Very few Crusaders escaped. Many were killed and many were captured. Among the prisoners were King Guy and Reynold of Châtillon, who was known as Arnat by the Moslems. Reynold had spent 16 years as a prisoner of the Moslems. When he was freed he attacked his enemies whenever he could. He even attacked and sank a boatful of Moslem pilgrims travelling to Mecca. Baha ad-Din wrote that 'The villain Arnat was a powerful and violent infidel. During a truce he attacked a caravan of Moslem traders and captured it. He tortured the men and imprisoned them in narrow dungeons.'

Source M

A medieval artist's interpretation of the loss of the True Cross (one of the holiest Christian relics) at the Battle of Hattin. He may have read the story in source K.

EVIDENCE: THE BATTLE OF HATTIN

1 How useful is source K for investigating the events of the battle?
2 How useful is source J for investigating the reasons why the Crusaders were beaten?
3 Which of the sources is most useful for investigating (a) what happened in the battle, (b) the reasons why the Moslems won? Explain the reasons for your choices.
4 Is source M a reliable source of evidence about the battle? Explain your answer.
5 Why did Saladin win the Battle of Hattin?
6 What would you have advised Saladin to do with a King Guy and b Reynold of Châtillon? Choose from the list of options and explain your choice.
   i   execute him
   ii put him in prison
   iii set him free

After the Battle

'When all the prisoners had been taken, Saladin went to his tent and sent for the King of the Franks and Prince Arnat (Reynold of Châtillon). He had the King seated beside him and, as he was half-dead with thirst, gave him iced water to drink. The King drank and gave the rest to Arnat, who also drank. Saladin said "This godless man did not have my permission to drink and will not save his life that way". He turned on Arnat and listed all his crimes and sins.

Then, with his own hand, he cut off the man's head. "Twice" said Saladin, "I have sworn to kill that man. Once when he attacked Mecca and Medina and again when he broke the truce and attacked the caravan."'

That account was written by Ibn al-Athir. Imad ad-Din gives more details, telling how Reynold defiantly answered Saladin and King Guy shook with fear because he expected to be killed next.

Many captives from the battle were sold as slaves. This picture shows a Moslem slave market.

In fact Guy was safe as soon as Saladin gave him a drink, because to Moslems this meant he became a guest who could not be harmed. However, Saladin did not give Reynold a drink because he intended to execute him.

Saladin treated Guy well because he was a king. Reynold was executed because he had attacked the holy places of Islam, pilgrims and had broken the truce — a promise of peace. Saladin also ordered the execution of all the Knights Templar and Knights Hospitaller, for the soldier-priests were the greatest enemies of the Moslems. The other prisoners were ransomed or became slaves. There were so many slaves that they could be bought very cheaply. One was even swapped for a shoe.

The capture of Jerusalem

The Christians no longer had an army to defend their kingdom. Saladin's army moved on, taking town after town, until it reached Jerusalem. Jerusalem was full of refugees, mainly women and children. There was only a handful of soldiers to defend the city and it soon surrendered on 2 October 1187.

The Moslems took Christian crosses down from the mosques but there was no other looting or destruction in the city. There was no revenge for the way the Crusaders had treated the Moslem holy places in 1099. Richer prisoners were set free after paying ransoms. Saladin let many of the poor go free without a ransom but many others became slaves. Christians were not forced to leave Jerusalem. The native people who were Christians were allowed to stay and worship in the churches. Saladin also invited the Jews to return to Jerusalem.

The events of 1187
June 30
Saladin and his army crossed the River Jordan
July 4
Battle of Hattin
October 2
Saladin and Moslem forces captured Jerusalem
October 29
The Pope proclaimed the Third Crusade
November
Richard of England took the Cross

The capture of Jerusalem by Saladin in 1187.

Saladin's plans and tactics in war

The greater size of the Moslem army

Why were the Moslems successful?

Saladin's leadership which united the Moslems

Moslem soldiers were more used to the heat and geography of the area

The Crusaders often quarrelled amongst themselves

Source N

The Sultan Saladin won possession of Jerusalem on the anniversary of the ascension of the Holy Prophet into heaven from Jerusalem. God allowed the Moslems to take the city as a celebration of the anniversary of the Holy Prophet's midnight journey. Truly this is a sign that this deed was pleasing to Almighty God.

(Al-Qadi al-Fadil, one of Saladin's advisers and councillors)

Source O

Long ago when our soldiers took Jerusalem they built a stone cross above the wall. The savage Moslem horde demolished this. It was as though the weapons and engines of war were telling of God's anger and the doom of the city. Glorious was Jerusalem, the city of God, but she is now contaminated by her enemy.

(From *The Journey of King Richard*, written in the early 1200's and based on eyewitness accounts)

CAUSES AND CONSEQUENCES: SALADIN'S VICTORIES

In this chapter you have read about Saladin himself and the reasons why he won the Battle of Hattin and captured Jerusalem. On the right are five reasons why he was successful. Which of them was the most important reason for his success? Explain the reasons for your choice.

a   The Crusaders often quarrelled among themselves.
b   Saladin's plans and tactics in war.
c   Saladin's leadership, which united the Moslems.
d   The greater size of the Moslem army.
e   Moslem soldiers were more used to the heat and geography of the area.

The most famous Crusade

● Frederick Barbarossa, Holy Roman Emperor, was nearly 70 when he set off on Crusade. He had been on the Second Crusade 40 years earlier, but had spent all the intervening years defending his huge empire. He was a famous soldier, much feared by Saladin and other Moslem leaders. His nickname came from his long, red beard: Barba-rossa.

● Son of Henry II, Richard was the greatest soldier in Europe. He became king in 1189 but had

Richard I

already been fighting to defend his lands in Aquitaine (the south of France) for years. He and Philip knew each other well and did not trust each other.

● Philip had been King of France since 1180. He was very clever and cunning and had spent ten years trying to outwit Henry II of England. England and France were rivals because the huge Angevin Empire, ruled by the Kings of England, lay next to France and Philip claimed to own some of the land.

The news that Saladin had captured Jerusalem reached Europe very quickly. Pope Urban III was said to have died of shock when he heard the news. In every country people promised to go on Crusade to win back Jerusalem for the Christians. This chapter will investigate why the Third Crusade did not recapture Jerusalem, despite this enthusiasm.

Why couldn't the Crusaders re-capture Jerusalem?

The shock and horror at the loss of Jerusalem was so great that Christians in Europe believed stories like the one described in Source A. They still had no idea that Jerusalem was a holy city for the Moslems too. Even kings volunteered to go on the new crusade. Previously kings had stayed at home to guard their lands but now three kings agreed to go on Pope Gregory VIII's Crusade —

Henry II of England and his eldest son, Richard, Philip II of France and Frederick Barbarossa of the Holy Roman Empire.

Source A

The Marquis of Montferrat, one of the most cunning Franks, was chiefly responsible for luring crowds of Crusaders from overseas. He had a picture painted showing the Church of the Resurrection in Jerusalem and the tomb where the Messiah was buried. The picture showed a Moslem knight trampling the tomb, over which his horse was urinating. This picture was sent abroad, priests carried it about and in this way they raised a huge army.

(Baha ad-Din, the biographer of Saladin)

Source B

Josias, Archbishop of Tyre, preached the word of God to the kings and princes in a wonderful way and turned their hearts to taking up the cross. Those who had been enemies were made friends. As the kings of France and England received the cross from his hands the sign of the cross appeared in the sky. When they saw this miracle, many rushed to take the cross.

(Roger of Howden, an English chronicler. He worked for Henry II and went on Crusade with Richard I)

Despite this miracle, the Crusade was delayed by quarrels between England and France and by the death of Henry II. The new king, Richard I, had to make sure his huge Angevin empire (which reached from south-west France to the Scottish border) was safe before he could set off. Eventually, Frederick Barbarossa began his crusade without waiting for Richard or Philip.

EVIDENCE: THE BEGINNING OF THE THIRD CRUSADE

1 Is source A reliable evidence of the way Crusaders were recruited? Explain your answer.

2 Does source B contain any reliable evidence about the beginning of the Crusade? Explain your answer.

3 Some of the information in sources A and B is wrong or exaggerated. Does this mean that these sources are completely useless for historians? Explain your answer.

4 Many people expected this Crusade to be successful.
  a Why did they expect it to be successful?
  b What were the possible weaknesses of this Crusade?

⚜ Problems for the Crusaders

By the time Richard and Philip set off on Crusade their task was already more difficult. Saladin had captured 50 more Crusader castles. The Christians only held three — Tyre, Tripoli and Antioch. If Saladin had taken the risk of attacking Tyre it might have been captured as well.

Even worse news soon reached Richard and Philip. Frederick Barbarossa had almost reached the Holy Land when he was drowned trying to swim across a river. Most of his huge army turned round and headed home. Only a few carried on to join the other Crusaders. Saladin was very relieved when he heard the news. He knew the Crusaders were much weaker now.

There were other problems, too, before the Crusaders reached the Holy Land. Richard attacked the town of Messina in Sicily to help his sister, Joan, who had been Queen of Sicily until her husband died. Richard and Philip quarrelled over Messina's captured treasure. Later, Richard captured Cyprus after its ruler imprisoned shipwrecked Crusaders. Therefore, Richard did not land at Acre in the Holy Land until June 1191, four years after Saladin had captured Jerusalem. Do you think these events strengthened or weakened the Crusaders' chance of success?

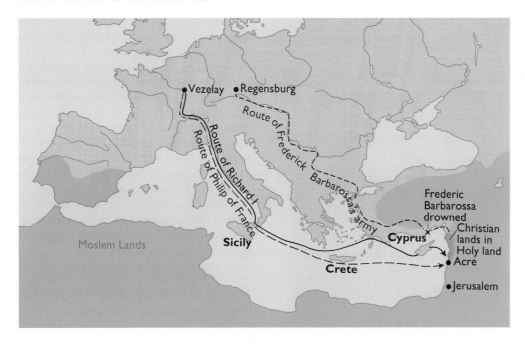

The routes taken by the Crusaders.

Source C

On 4 October 1190 Richard I captured Messina with a single attack in less time than a priest would take to sing matins. Many more citizens would have perished if the king in his mercy had not given orders to spare them. The English seized all the gold, silver and valuables they could find. Suddenly, the French noticed Richard's flags flying above the city walls. Philip II of France was outraged and his jealousy lasted all his life. Philip's counsellors advised him to make Richard remove his flags. Richard was furious but at last his anger cooled. He would not bow to enemy soldiers but he yielded to soft words. The banners of both kings were raised above the walls.

(From *The Journey of King Richard*, written in the early 1200's by an English churchman. It was based on eye-witness accounts)

Source D

Richard landed with his army at Acre. The earth shook with the joy of the Christians. Everyone rejoiced and there were fanfares and trumpets. Everyone was glad, for the arrival of the king had been long wished for by all people.

(From *The Journey of King Richard*)

The Siege of Acre

Richard joined the siege of Acre, where the Moslems held the city. King Guy of Jerusalem had already been besieging Acre for 2 years but, after Richard's arrival, it took only another 4 weeks to capture the city. An English chronicler wrote a long account of the end of the siege which includes the extracts on the right.

The most horrific weapon was Greek fire. Both armies mixed chemicals to produce flames that were almost impossible to put out.

Source E

The King of France, not wanting delay, told King Richard that the time was right for an attack. However, Richard said that he was not ready. He was seriously ill and some of his men had not yet arrived. He hoped that they would arrive with the next fleet and bring material for building siege machinery. The King of France did not give up his idea of attacking. Violent battle began but the French could not attack the city and, at the same time, defend themselves from attacks by the Moslems outside the town. Many were killed by spears, stones from ballistas and the spreading of Greek fire. After the French attack ended, the Moslem soldiers destroyed the siege engines with Greek fire. The French king was so overcome with rage, so it is said, that he fell into a fit of melancholy and, in his confusion and desolation, would not even mount a horse.

King Richard had not fully recovered from his illness but he was anxious to capture the city. He had himself carried out on a silken litter so that he could encourage his men and frighten the Moslems by his appearance. His ballistas killed many men with missiles and spears. His miners made an underground passage to the tower his engines were firing at. They hacked out the foundations of the tower, filled the hole with timber and set fire to it. Then the stone missiles helped to knock the tower to bits. King Richard pondered the difficulties of the siege and the bravery of the enemy. He decided he would encourage the young soldiers with rewards rather than with commands. He promised four gold pieces to anyone who removed a stone from the walls of Acre. The men, inspired with great courage, overcame danger and removed a great many stones from the massive wall.

Shortly afterwards, the Moslem forces in Acre surrendered. The Crusaders now had an important base for the rest of their expedition. Ships from Europe or Cyprus could bring supplies of food, equipment and men into Acre.

Source F

While the Crusaders besieged the Moslem defenders in Acre they were themselves besieged by Saladin's army. The Christian army was so short of food that the soldiers were eating dogs when the new arrivals appeared. This is a medieval artist's impression of the siege.

EVIDENCE: THE SIEGE OF ACRE

1 Is source E a useful source for historians about **a** the events of the siege, **b** King Richard? Explain your answer.
2 Are pictures such as source F more or less useful than written accounts for historians investigating warfare during the Crusades?
3 What questions would you ask about source E to help you decide whether it is a reliable source?
4 'Source F is unreliable because it shows Moslem soldiers in western armour. Therefore, historians cannot learn anything from it.'
   Explain why you agree or disagree with this statement.

The Battle of Arsuf

The capture of Acre was a great victory but it could have been the end of the Crusade. Philip of France decided to return home. He was sick and also worried that enemies might attack France. He did not get on well with Richard and the French and English armies were rivals as well as allies. At the end of July 1191 he sailed for home. Originally, the Crusade had been led by three great kings. Now there was only one left.

Richard decided to stay and fight on, although he too was worried about his lands. At the end of August 1191 he led his army out of Acre on the march towards Jerusalem. After days of difficult travel they were attacked by Saladin's Moslem army at Arsuf. The Crusaders beat off the attack but they were almost defeated. Some of Richard's knights almost lost the battle by charging too soon. Richard had to lead the rest into the charge before he was ready but he still drove off the Moslems. After this victory Richard seemed very close to capturing Jerusalem.

Look at the sources on this page and think about your work so far. Do you think that Richard had a good chance of capturing Jerusalem?

Source G

The Moslems, unlike our men, are not weighed down with armour, so they are able to advance more quickly. They are almost unarmed as they carry only a bow, a spiked club, a sword, a reed lance tipped with iron and a loose-slung knife. If they are driven off they flee on very swift horses, the fastest in the world, like swallows in flight. They also have a trick of halting their flight when the pursuers give up the chase. Then they attack you again.

(*The Journey of King Richard*, written in the early 1200's and based on eye-witness accounts)

Source H

The King, seeing his men break away
From line and charge into the fray,
At once drove his spurs into his steed
And forced him to his swiftest speed:
Charging without delay, he made
All haste to lend these first troops aid.
Swifter than crossbow bolt doth fly
He rode, with his bold company
Toward the right, where with fierce hand
He fell upon the pagan band
With such impetuous attack
That they were mazed and taken back
And from their saddles hurled and thrown,
So that like sheaves of grain thick strewn
Ye had seen them lying on the earth;
And England's king, of valiant worth,
Took after them and close pursued
Them, with such skill and fortitude
That round him all the road was filled
With Saracens who had been killed.

(From *The History of the Holy War* by Ambroise, a Norman churchman who wrote about what he saw on Crusade)

Richard's army formation when he marched from Acre to Jaffa in 1191.

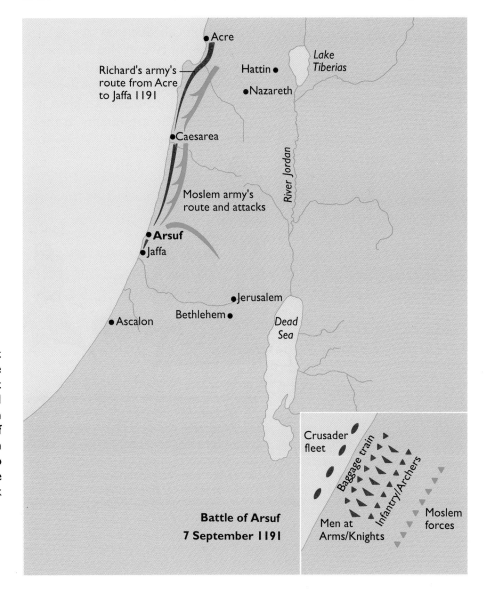

Battle of Arsuf
7 September 1191

The Third Crusade

1190
June 10
Frederick Barbarossa drowned
July
Richard I and Philip of France set off on Crusade
October
Capture of Messina in Sicily
1191
March
Capture of Cyprus
May
Philip sailed to Acre
June 8
Richard reached Acre
July 12
Crusaders captured Acre
September 7
Battle of Arsuf
1192
January
Richard close to Jerusalem but retreated
June
Richard close to Jerusalem but retreated again
August
Crusaders' defence of Jaffa
September
Treaty between Richard and Saladin

A western picture of Richard and Saladin agreeing the truce. However, they never actually met, although they sent gifts to each other. Saladin was said to have sent snow to cool Richard when he was ill.

The terms of the truce
- The Christians would have control of the coast between Acre and Jaffa
- Christians could freely visit their holy places in Jerusalem
- Trade could be carried on without attacks
- The defences of Ascalon (an important Crusader fortress) should be destroyed and not rebuilt for three years after Easter 1193

≋ Jerusalem

In fact Richard led his army towards Jerusalem twice. The first time, in January 1192, he camped just 12 miles away but conditions were very difficult. There was heavy rain which made travel hard. A strong Moslem army was nearby, ready to surround the Christians if they besieged Jerusalem. Even if the Christian army captured Jerusalem they would have difficulty defending it against the enemy.

Many in the Christian army were still eager to attack Jerusalem but most of the experienced leaders advised Richard to retreat. They marched away but only six months later, in June, they were back. Once again Richard and the other leaders faced a difficult decision. A committee of twenty leaders met and again advised Richard that, even if they captured Jerusalem, they would not be able to keep it. You can see the arguments in the chart on the right.

Richard had only seen Jerusalem from a distance after fighting so hard. In September 1192 he agreed a truce with Saladin and sailed for home.

Should you attack Jerusalem?

For
- Jerusalem was the Holy City for Christians.
- Many Crusaders, including Richard, had travelled hundreds of miles and had spent months fighting for the chance to capture Jerusalem.
- Victory would win a place in heaven.
- A piece of the True Cross had just been discovered – a good omen.

Against
- Many lives would be lost in the attack.
- It would be difficult to hold Jerusalem even if it was captured. The Moslem forces were much larger and would attack after Richard had left for home.
- The Crusaders' army might be caught between Jerusalem and the Moslem army.
- There was news from home of trouble in England.
- A stronger base for Christian action was needed. It would be better to conquer Egypt and strengthen the Christian cities before attacking Jerusalem.

THE DECISION AT JERUSALEM

1 Which was the most powerful reason for attacking Jerusalem? Explain your choice.
2 Which was the most powerful reason for retreating? Explain your choice.
3 Do you think it was a difficult decision for Richard and the other leaders? Explain your answer.
4 Do you think that their decision was right? Explain your answer.
5 Was the Crusade a success? Explain your answer.

Richard the Lionheart

Richard had not captured Jerusalem but the legend of Richard the Lionheart had begun. Moslem mothers told their children that the terrible Richard would come for them if they did not go to sleep. He is still one of the most famous English kings, thanks to the stories of the Crusaders and of Robin Hood. Is the legend based on truth?

Source I

King Richard, alone, berserk, came on the Moslems. No man could escape his sword. He made a clear path far and wide, wherever he went, as if mowing hay with a scythe. For half a mile the bodies of the dead lay face down on the ground.

(from *The Journey of King Richard*, written by an English churchman)

Source J

This King of England was courageous, energetic and daring in combat. When he arrived at Acre the Franks let out cries of joy. The hearts of the Moslems were filled with fear.

(Baha ad-Din, Saladin's secretary)

Source K

With many tears we offer our humble prayers, asking you to persuade the princes and nobles of Christendom to serve the living God so that after Easter they shall guard and defend the inheritance of God (Jerusalem) which we will, God willing, fully possess by Easter.

(Richard I writing to the Abbot of the monastery of Clairvaux in France in October 1191. Richard knew he would have to return home soon and was seeking reinforcements)

Source L

Saladin thought King Richard so pleasant, honest, magnanimous and excellent that, if his lands were lost, he would rather they belonged to Richard than to any other prince.

(*The Journey of King Richard*, describing Saladin's reaction after the truce had been agreed)

Source M

King Richard waited three weeks after the time when Saladin had said he would release the hostages and return the Holy Cross. Saladin did not return the Holy Cross and he neglected the hostages. Instead he sent gifts and messages, gaining time by false and clever words. He did not keep any of his promises. A council of the Crusaders' leaders agreed to behead the Moslem prisoners. King Richard ordered that 2,700 of the prisoners be led out of the city and executed.

(*The Journey of King Richard*, describing the execution of prisoners after the siege of Acre)

Source N

The English king broke his word to the Moslem prisoners who had surrendered the city in return for their lives. If the Sultan Saladin paid their ransom they were to be freed. If he did not they were to become slaves. When he saw that Saladin delayed payment he secretly changed his mind. Even after he received the money and the Frankish prisoners he ordered the cold-blooded slaughter of more than 3,000 men in chains.

(Baha ad-Din, Saladin's secretary, describing the same event as source M)

Although Richard is a great English hero he was not really English. He spoke little English and his favourite lands were in Aquitaine in the south of France. He was king of England for 10 years but spent little time there, choosing intelligent men to run the country for him.

EVIDENCE: RICHARD THE LIONHEART

1 Read sources I and J. Which source gives more reliable evidence about Richard's bravery and skill as a soldier? Explain your answer.
2 Do you think that Richard was a religious man? Use source K and any other evidence to support your answer.
3 Is source L useful evidence about Richard? Explain your answer.
4 Sources M and N describe the same event. Which of them is the more reliable account of the deaths of the prisoners? Explain your choice.
5 Sources M and N are reliable evidence about **a** the executions, **b** Richard's attitudes to prisoners, **c** the kind of propaganda produced by both sides. Explain which of these statements you agree with.
6 Write your own description of Richard's character and abilities, using the sources on this page and any other evidence you have.

Why didn't they capture Jerusalem?

In chapters 3 and 4 you have investigated some of the main events of the Third Crusade and the characters of the two leaders, Saladin and Richard. You have also read about some of the reasons why the Crusaders did not capture Jerusalem. Now you need to put all these ideas together to explain why the Crusaders did not capture Jerusalem.

Crusader knights in battle with Moslem horsemen

Source O

Why were our fathers, although only a small force, able to destroy the multitudes of the enemy when the men of our own times have often been conquered? The first reason is that our forefathers were religious men who feared God. Now a wicked generation has grown up sinful sons and the Lord has withdrawn his favour.

A second reason is that earlier Crusaders were trained in battle and familiar in the use of weapons. The Christians of the East, however, because of a long peace, became unused to war and gloried in their inactivity. A third reason is that nowadays all the Moslem kingdoms around us obey only one leader and, however reluctantly, they are ready as one unit to take up arms.

(William of Tyre, 1130–1185, who spent most of his life in the kingdom of Jerusalem and was Archbishop of Tyre)

CAUSES AND CONSEQUENCES: WHY DID THE CRUSADERS FAIL TO CAPTURE JERUSALEM?

1 Use the information on this page and in the rest of chapters 3 and 4. List the reasons why Richard and the Crusaders failed to capture Jerusalem.

2 Which was the most important reason for their failure? Explain your choice.
3 Write your own explanation of why the Crusaders did not capture Jerusalem.

Was the Crusade really a failure?

Richard and the Crusaders did not capture Jerusalem but that does not mean the Crusade was a failure. Certainly Saladin and the Moslems still held the Holy City but the Crusaders had achieved some successes. Look at source P and the diagram below, which shows the results of the Third Crusade. Do you think it was a success or a failure? What evidence would you use to support your answer?

William of Tyre, one of the most well-informed chroniclers, who wrote his account between 1169 and 1173

The Moslems still held Jerusalem and surrounded the Christian lands

The Moslem advance had been stopped

Victories at Arsuf and Jaffa inspired many Christians

The results of the Third Crusade

The Christian leaders still had a chance of capturing Egypt as the base for the next attack on the Moslem armies

The truce confirmed that the Christians had regained land and pilgrims were allowed to visit Jerusalem

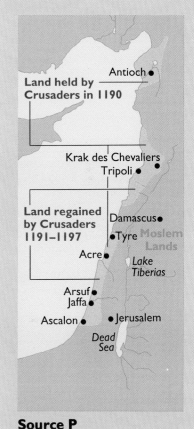

Source P

The lands recovered as a result of the Third Crusade

USING SOURCES AS EVIDENCE

In this chapter you have used a lot of sources. You have read Moslem and Christian writers and seen pictures of the events described. Historians cannot work without sources but they do not just copy out what the sources say. What have you learned about using sources as evidence?

1 Explain why you agree or disagree with each of these statements:

a Historians should always believe sources written at the time of the event they describe

b Historians should always disbelieve what Moslem writers say about Crusaders

c Historians always need to check what a writer says by reading other sources

d Historians do not need to check what was written by priests

e Written sources always give more valuable evidence than pictures.

2 What questions would you ask about a source to check if it is reliable?

3 Medieval artists were not very good at drawing people so their pictures are not useful to historians. Explain why you agree or disagree with this statement.

The Crusades: change and continuity

So far, you have investigated the Crusades in the 1100's, especially the Third Crusade. This Crusade, which tried to recapture Jerusalem, is the most famous because of Richard and Saladin. Those are the events people think of when they hear the word 'Crusades' — but were all Crusades like the ones you have been reading about?

In the chart below you can see 6 statements about the Crusades. This chapter will help you decide whether they are true or whether they should be altered. By the end

of the chapter you will know whether the Crusades were all the same or whether there were changes as the years went by.

Copy this chart. Put a tick in the first column if you agree with the statement, a cross if you do not agree. Then work through pages 35–39, putting evidence about each statement in the second column. At the end of each section fill in column 3 with a tick or a cross. Were you right first time or did the evidence make you change your mind?

	First idea ✓ or ✗	Evidence about the statement	Answer after looking at the evidence ✓ or ✗
The Crusades were wars fought between Christians and Moslems			
They were always fought in the Holy Land to control Jerusalem			
The Crusades lasted 100 years but died out after Richard's Crusade			
The Crusaders were kings and knights			
People went on Crusade because they were very religious			
Everyone in Europe supported the Crusades			

℮ Who, where and when?

The information on page 35 will help you think about the first 3 statements in your chart. Take each statement in turn and look for evidence that will help you decide whether it is right or wrong.

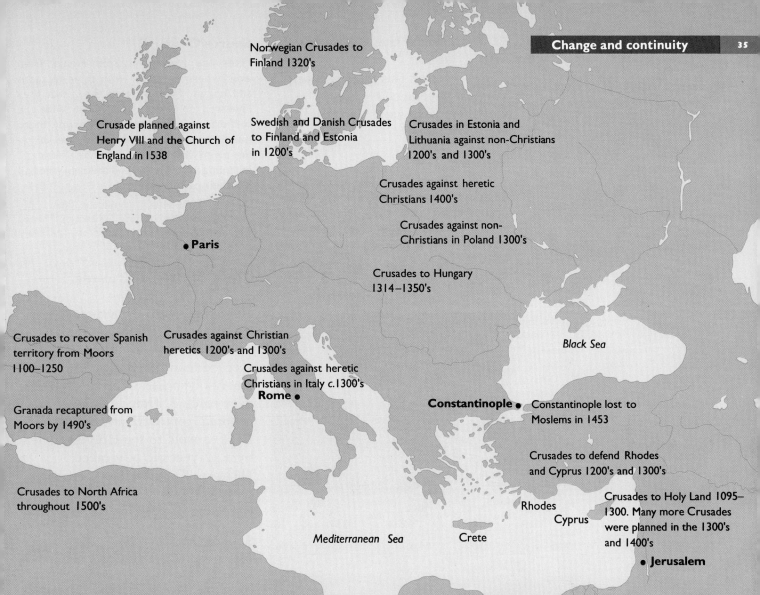

Norwegian Crusades to
Finland 1320's

Crusade planned against
Henry VIII and the Church of
England in 1538

Swedish and Danish Crusades
to Finland and Estonia
in 1200's

Crusades in Estonia and
Lithuania against non-Christians
1200's and 1300's

Crusades against heretic
Christians 1400's

Crusades against non-
Christians in Poland 1300's

Crusades to Hungary
1314–1350's

• Paris

Black Sea

Crusades to recover Spanish
territory from Moors
1100–1250

Crusades against Christian
heretics 1200's and 1300's

Crusades against heretic
Christians in Italy c.1300's
Rome •

Granada recaptured from
Moors by 1490's

Constantinople • Constantinople lost to
Moslems in 1453

Crusades to defend Rhodes
and Cyprus 1200's and 1300's

Crusades to North Africa
throughout 1500's

Rhodes

Cyprus

Crusades to Holy Land 1095–
1300. Many more Crusades
were planned in the 1300's
and 1400's

Mediterranean Sea

Crete

• Jerusalem

Crusades to Egypt to win base
for attack on Holy and in 1200's

This map give a brief summary of
the Crusades

Source A

When we took Alexandria, he was there.
He often sat at table in the chair
Of honour, above all nations, when in
Prussia.
In Lithuania he had ridden, and Russia,
No Christian man so often, of his rank.
When, in Granada, Algerians sank
Under assault, he had been there, and in
North Africa, raiding Benamarin;
In Anatolia he had been as well

And fought when Ayas and Anatolia fell,
For all along the Mediterranean coast
He had embarked with many a noble host.
In fifteen mortal battles had he been
And jousted for our faith at Tramissene.

(From Geoffrey Chaucer's *The Canterbury
Tales*, written in the late 1300's. These lines tell
of the places where the Knight in the Tales had
fought)

Peter the Hermit, the leader of the People's Crusade in 1096

✋ Who were the Crusaders?

The sources on this page will help you test statement 4 – 'The Crusaders were kings and knights, not poor people'.

Source B

An observant old soldier told me that on the other side of the defences was a woman dressed in a green mantle, who shot at us with a wooden bow and wounded many Moslems before she was overcome and killed.

(Baha ad-Din, describing the siege of Acre in 1191)

Source C

Peter the Hermit inspired Franks from everywhere to gather with their weapons and horses. They were so eager that they appeared on every road. Along with the soldiers was an unarmed crowd, more numerous than the sand or the stars, carrying palms and crosses on their shoulders, including even women and children who had left their own countries.

(An eyewitness description of Peter the Hermit's Crusaders in 1096, written by Anna Comnena, daughter of the Emperor Alexius of Constantinople)

The Children's Crusade

After the Fourth Crusade failed, many people said that innocent children were more likely to succeed than the priests, kings and knights who had failed to do their duty to God. Thousands of children from Germany set off in 1212 to walk to the Holy Land, led by a 12 year old boy called Nicholas. Only the lucky ones returned home. The rest died or were sold as slaves.

Source D

Boys and girls, and some men and women, set out with him, all penniless. Nobody could stop them, neither their parents nor their friends. People did anything to join the expedition. As it passed by, people put down their tools or whatever they had in their hands at the time and joined in.

(The Annals of Marbach, describing the beginning of the Children's Crusade in 1212. The chronicle was written shortly afterwards)

Source E

Many women went on Crusade with their husbands or on their own. One chronicle records the death of a woman during the siege of Acre. She had been carrying soil to build an earthwork when she was wounded by a spear. Before she died, she begged her husband to use her body as part of the mound to help with the building.

Source F

Knights embarking for the Crusades

℮ Why did they go on Crusade?

Did people go on Crusade just because of religion? Did people go for other reasons completely? These sources will help you think about the motives of the Crusaders.

Source G

- The property and family of Crusaders were protected while they were away.
- Crusaders were free from taxes until they returned.
- Crusaders' debts need not be paid until they returned.
- Going on Crusade wiped out all earlier sins. Anyone killed on Crusade was certain of a place in heaven.

(Some of the rights of Crusaders listed by the Pope in 1215)

Source J

Forever will we weave silk,
But never will we be well dressed,
Forever we'll be poor and naked,
Forever will we hunger and thirst
But the man we toil for
Gets rich because of us.

(Chrétien de Troyes, a 12th century poet, describing the attitudes of young workers in towns who were attracted by the adventure of the Crusades)

Source K

A messenger of hell has risen, the false prophet Muhammad, who has seduced many men from the truth. Although his treachery has been successful until now, we put our trust in the Lord who has given us a sign that good will triumph.

(From a letter sent by the Pope in 1213)

Nearly everyone worked on the land and it was often hard, back-breaking work. Some Crusaders must have gone to escape this drudgery at home.

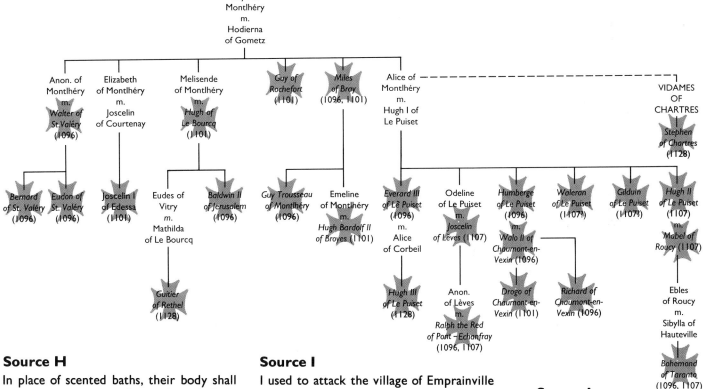

Source H

In place of scented baths, their body shall have a narrow pit in the earth, and there they shall have a bath more black and foul than any bath of pitch and sulphur. In place of a soft couch they shall have a bed more grievous and hard than all the nails and spikes in the world. Instead of wives they shall have toads. Instead of a throng of followers, their body shall have a throng of worms. They shall have eternal torment.

(A description of hell in a fourteenth century sermon by Friar John Bromyard)

Source I

I used to attack the village of Emprainville with a troop of my knights and take the goods of the monks and give them to my knights. In order to obtain the pardon which God can give me for my crimes, I am going on pilgrimage to Jerusalem which has been enslaved with her sons. The monks have given me ten pounds towards the expenses in return for giving up my harsh treatment of them.

(Nivelo of Freteval, before going on Crusade, 1096)

Source L

Many family groups went on Crusade – brothers, cousins and people related by marriage. This chart shows a remarkable example of a Crusader family from France.

Edward I

Later Crusading Kings

● Louis IX, King of France 1226–1270. He led two Crusades but was taken prisoner at Mansourah in 1249 and died leading his second crusade in 1270. He was canonized as a Saint in 1297 for his lifelong devotion to Crusading and the fight for Jerusalem.

● Edward I of England, 1272–1307. Edward went on Crusade to the Holy Land in 1270 and was away from England when his father, Henry III, died in 1272. Edward eventually returned in 1274.

● Henry IV of England, 1399–1413. Henry was one of the most famous soldiers in Europe before he became king. He went on Crusade to North Africa and Lithuania before making a pilgrimage to Jerusalem in 1392.

● Henry VIII was almost on the receiving end of a Crusade. After he quarrelled with the Pope and started the Church of England, the Pope tried to persuade the Kings of Spain and France to lead a Crusade against England. The Spanish Armada in 1588 was a Crusade by the Catholic Philip of Spain against the Protestant Queen Elizabeth.

Did everyone support the Crusaders?

We know that many thousands of people went on Crusades. There were rich and poor, men, women and children. Many travelled as soldier-pilgrims, some just to visit the Holy Land. Clearly the idea of crusading was very popular but was there criticism of crusading? Did crusading remain popular and important for long after Richard's Crusade in the 1190s?

Source L

The priests and other sensible people spoke against the expedition and said it was useless. But people accused the priests of being unbelievers and jealous.

(The Annals of Marbach, a chronicle in the early 1200s, describing reactions to the Children's Crusade)

Source M

You fools cross the sea, spend all your money, expose your life to many dangers, while I remain with my wife and children because I redeemed my Crusading vow for five marks. Yet I shall receive the same reward in heaven as you.

(Caesarius of Heisterbach, about 1235)

Source N

War is not effective against the Moslems because those who survive, together with their children are more and more embittered against the Christian faith.

(Roger Bacon, 1260)

Source O

There was no nation so remote, no people so retired that they did not contribute to the Crusades. The Welshman left his hunting, the Scot his fellowship with lice, the Dane his drinking party, the Norwegian his warship. Lands were deserted by their farmers, houses by their inhabitants.

(William of Malmesbury, writing in the early 1100s)

Source P

God is not pleased with a forced service. Whoever seeks to spread the faith through violence goes against our religion.

(Ralph Niger, writing in the 1180s)

Source Q

To fight in defence of justice against both unbelievers and Christians is holy and permissible. Some say that Christians are not allowed to fight against unbelievers. This opinion is false and wrong. First, it would not permit any Christian king to defend his kingdom against invaders. Secondly, the teaching of the Holy Fathers has approved and vindicated just wars if they are to defend justice or protect the church and faith. God himself has upheld just wars of this kind and indeed often ordered his chosen people to fight.

(William Colwyll and John Netton, replying to critics of the Crusaders in the 1380s)

Source R

Thus were it good to set all in even,
The world's princes and priests both,
For love of him which is the king of heaven,
The Saracens who unto Christ are loathe,
Let men be armed against them to fight
So may the knight his deed of arms right.

(John Gower's address to Henry IV of England, c.1400)

Source S

An unjust war, in which greed was the spur to action rather than the extermination of the unbeliever.

(Roger of Wendover, an English chronicler, writing about the Crusade against Christian heretics in southern France in the 1220s. Christians who changed their ideas and disagreed with the Pope, even about small details, were called heretics and were attacked)

Source T

Rhys ap Gruffydd was quite determined to make the Holy journey to Jerusalem. He spent a fortnight energetically preparing for the journey, collecting pack animals and persuading other men to go with him. Then his wife, Gwenllian put a sudden stop to his noble intentions.

At Abergavenny many men took the cross. The Archbishop asked a nobleman called Arthenus if he would take the cross. He answered, 'I cannot take such a step without consulting my friends'. 'Shouldn't you ask your wife?' asked the Archbishop. Arthenus looked down at the ground with some embarrassment and said, 'This is man's work we are considering. There is no point in asking the advice of a woman.' Then he took the cross without further delay.

(Extracts from *The Journey through Wales* by Gerald of Wales. Gerald travelled round Wales with the Archbishop of Canterbury in 1188 to preach the Crusade after Saladin had captured Jerusalem)

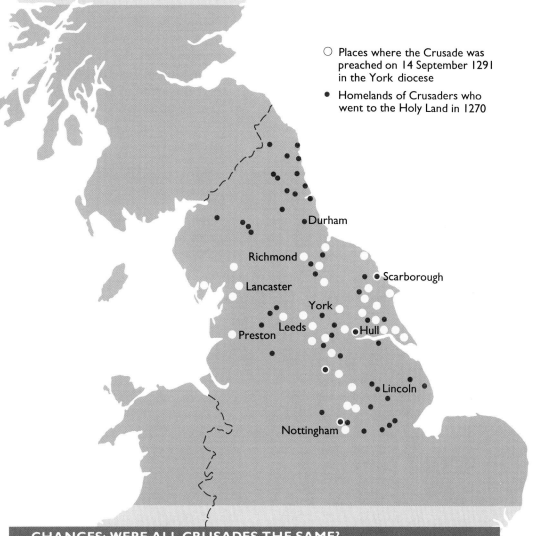

○ Places where the Crusade was preached on 14 September 1291 in the York diocese

● Homelands of Crusaders who went to the Holy Land in 1270

Durham
Richmond
Lancaster
Scarborough
York
Preston Leeds Hull
Lincoln
Nottingham

Source U

This map shows the home lands of northerners who went on Crusade with Prince Edward (later Edward I) in 1270, and the places where another Crusade was preached on 14 September 1291. The Archbishop of York sent friars all over the north to preach on the same day.

CHANGES: WERE ALL CRUSADES THE SAME?

You now have plenty of evidence in your chart. This evidence will help you decide whether the six statements on page 34 were correct. The evidence will help you work out whether all Crusades were the same and what changed or stayed the same over the years.

1 Write 6 new statements answering the questions below
  a Who did the Crusaders fight against?
  b Where did they fight?
  c How long did the Crusades last?
  d Who were the Crusaders?
  e Why did people go on Crusades?
  f Did everyone support the Crusades?

2 Look at your evidence.
  a Which aspects of the Crusades stayed the same?
  b Which aspects of the Crusades changed?

3 Were all Crusades the same?

What can we learn from the Crusades?

Why did the Moslems keep control of Jerusalem?

Perhaps because they had better and larger armies.

▲ **Stage 1**

Historians begin with a question and a hypothesis.

This book gives several more reasons.

William of Tyre said the Christians were to blame for quarrelling amongst themselves.

▲ **Stage 2**

Historians check their hypothesis by looking at sources to find evidence.

I need to rewrite my answer – it was too simple the first time.

Have you seen this book? The writer has come up with some new ideas.

▲ **Stage 3**

Historians change or amend their hypothesis after looking at the evidence. Often new evidence can be found, even hundreds of years after an event.

How do we study history?

Historians try to answer questions about the past. Some questions are 'what happened?' questions like 'what did Pope Urban do in 1095?' or 'when did the Crusaders capture Jerusalem?' However, historians also ask more complicated questions about why events happened, what their consequences were and whether life changed or stayed the same.

Whatever the question is, historians follow the process that you have followed in this book and you can see in the chart on the left. What are the advantages of this way of working?

In the illustration below you can see some of the kinds of questions historians ask about the past. Here are four statements. Can you explain why each of them is wrong. You could use examples from your work on the Crusades to help you.

i The causes of an event are all equally important.
ii You cannot have change and continuity at the same time.
iii Everyone in the Middle Ages had the same ideas and beliefs.
iv Sources that tell the truth about one thing can be trusted about other details.

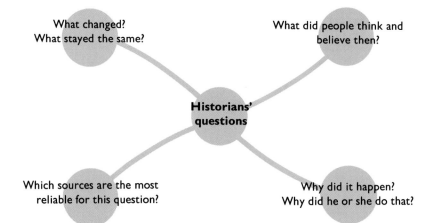

What changed? What stayed the same?

What did people think and believe then?

Historians' questions

Which sources are the most reliable for this question?

Why did it happen? Why did he or she do that?

🎏 Different Views

Historians investigating the past do not always agree with each other. They often have different views about why something happened or what a person was like. The Crusades is a good topic for helping to understand why historians disagree. The next 2 pages look at historians' opinions and disagreements about why the Crusaders failed and what Saladin was like. First, do you know the difference between FACTS – that historians do agree about – and

OPINIONS that they may disagree about? Which of the statements below are facts and which are opinions?

a Richard I was a better leader than Saladin.
b The Moslems captured Jerusalem in 1187.
c Many people went on Crusade because they were very religious.
d Saladin was right to execute Reynold of Châtillon.

Different views: the failure of the Crusades?

The later Crusades began when Jerusalem was captured by the Moslems in 1187. Recapturing Jerusalem was always the main aim of these Crusaders to the Holy Land. After the days of Richard I many more Crusades, both large and small, took place, but none of them succeeded in recapturing Jerusalem. Why not? Sources A and B give explanations for this failure.

Source A

Why were our fathers, although only a small force, able to destroy the multitudes of the enemy when the men of our own times have often been conquered? The first reason is that our forefathers were religious men who feared God. Now a wicked generation has grown up sinful sons and the Lord has withdrawn his favour.

A second reason is that earlier Crusaders were trained in battle and familiar in the use of weapons. The Christians of the East, however, because of a long peace, became unused to war and gloried in their inactivity. A third reason is that nowadays all the Moslem kingdoms around us obey only one leader and, however reluctantly, they are ready as one unit to take up arms.

(William of Tyre, 1130–1185. He was Archbishop of Tyre and spent most of his life in the Holy Land)

The capture of Jerusalem in 1099, showing siege weapons used by the Crusaders.

Source B

How can one account for the failure of Pope Gregory's plans (in the 1270s) and the fact that it proved impossible ever again to mount a really large international crusade of the old type? In the first place, the costs of warfare were rising and countries were less willing to co-operate, making old-fashioned crusades impracticable. Secondly, in the 1270s large scale crusades were not needed. Christians in the East needed a permanent garrison defence, not the spasmodic arrival of large bodies of troops who, after thoroughly upsetting the Moslems, would depart, leaving the original defenders to their fate. The fact was that the phenomenal success in 1099 had led to the belief that it was possible to send successful expeditions to the Holy Land. This was an illusion for the countries of Europe never had the resources or planning ability to succeed.

(J. Riley-Smith, *The Atlas of the Crusades*, 1991)

DIFFERENT VIEWS: WHY DID THE CRUSADES FAIL?

1 What reasons does source A give for the failure to recapture Jerusalem?
2 What reasons does source B give for the failure to recapture Jerusalem?
3 Which source gives the better explanation? Give reasons for your choice.
4 Why do you think the two writers give different explanations?

5 Do you think each of these people believed the Crusades were a success or a failure? Explain your answers.
   a Godfrey, first King of Jerusalem
   b Saladin
   c Richard I of England
   d Louis IX of France.
6 The Christian kingdom of Jerusalem survived for 300 years. Do you think that was a failure?

A European portrait of Saladin. What does this tell you about European understanding of life in the east?

Different views of Saladin

There are different answers to the question about the success or failure of the Crusades. They are different for a number of reasons that you can see in the diagram below. There can also be different views about people in history. Here is a group of sources about the Moslem leader, Saladin.

Historians might disagree because they use different sources

Historians might disagree because they like different people from the past

Writers in the past were closer to events than historians today. This can produce disagreements

Different views about the past

Historians might disagree because they choose different parts of the same source (see Source A, page 41)

Historians today might disagree with writers in the past because they have more evidence today

Historians might disagree because they are from different religions, countries or backgrounds

Source C

Once during the siege, when I was riding at the Sultan Saladin's side against the Franks, an army scout came to us with a sobbing woman. 'She came from the Frankish garrison', the scout explained, 'and wants to see the master. We brought her here.' Saladin asked the interpreter to question her. She said 'Yesterday some Moslem thieves entered my tent and stole my little girl. I cried all night and our commanders told me that Saladin is merciful, go to him and ask for your daughter back. Thus I have come and I place all my hopes in you.' Saladin was touched and tears came to his eyes. He sent someone to the slave market to look for the girl, and less than an hour later a horseman arrived bearing the child on his shoulders. All those present wept. Thus was her daughter returned to her and she was escorted back to the camp of the Franks.

(From Baha ad-Din's biography of Saladin. Baha ad-Din was a member of Saladin's household)

Source D

Reynold was led into the presence of Saladin and that tyrant, either following the impulse of passion or jealous of the great excellence of the man, cut off with his own hand that aged head. All the knights Templar he ordered to be beheaded, wishing to exterminate those who were most valiant in battle.

(From *The Journey of King Richard*, written in the early 1200's by an English churchman and based on eye-witness accounts)

Source E

Every time he seized a Frankish castle or stronghold, Saladin allowed the enemy soldiers to seek refuge in Tyre, a city that therefore became so strong it could not be captured. In a sense Saladin organised the defence of Tyre against his own army.

(Ibn al Athir, 1160–1233. An Arab historian)

DIFFERENT VIEWS: SALADIN

1 How would you describe Saladin if you only had:
  a Source C? b Source D? c Source E?
2 Use these sources and any others you have. Write or record your own description of Saladin's character and behaviour.
3 Compare your description with a friend's description.
  a What are the differences between them?
  b Why are they different?
4 Think of a famous person alive today.
  a What disagreements are there about his or her character and behaviour?
  b Why do people disagree?

The Consequences of the Crusades

Another reason for studying the Crusades is that they were important events – but how important were they? Some events in history were more important than others. For example, World War One and World War Two were very important events. The invention of printing and the discovery of penicillin were also very important. Why do we say these events were important? On the right you can see a list that shows the different reasons why events may be important. Can you explain why the events boxed above the list were important?

Pages 43–46 investigate whether the Crusades were important. As you work through these pages, use the sources to decide whether the Crusades were important and why they were important. Did they:

● affect lots of people at the time?
● affect a wide area?
● have consequences that lasted a long time?
● affect different aspects of the way people lived?

You could also look for more evidence earlier in the book.

The growth of the Roman Empire

The Norman Conquest

The Black Death

The invention of cars and televisions

Why were events important?
● They affected a lot of people at the time
● Their effects lasted for many years or centuries
● They affected a wide area of the world
● They affected many aspects of people's lives

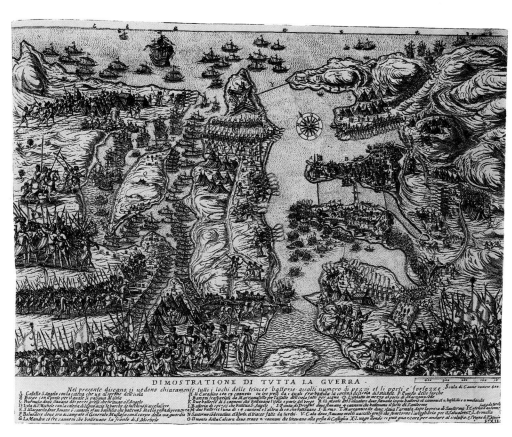

DIMOSTRATIONE DI TVTTA LA GVERRA.

Source F

By the sixteenth century Moslem forces had advanced across the Mediterranean. In 1565 they attacked the island of Malta and began a long siege. Once more the Pope called on the rulers of Europe to join together to defend Christianity, and a force of Italian and Spanish soldiers finally drove off the attackers. This picture shows the siege.

Source G

The Fourth Crusade went badly wrong. Instead of attacking Moslem lands, the Crusaders allied with the Venetians and destroyed the great Christian city of Constantinople. Here is one account of the looting: 'The Franks entered the town and next morning went into the church of Hagia Sophia and tore down the doors and cut them to pieces, together with the pulpit cased in silver and 12 silver pillars. They cut up the bracket and twelve crosses which hung over the altar, like trees taller than a man, and the altar rail because they were silver. They tore the precious stone and the great pearl from the marvellous altar and where they put the altar itself is not known.'

Source H

Belvoir castle was built near Tiberias in the Holy Land about 1170. Beaumaris was one of the castles built by Edward I to control Wales over a hundred years later. Castle building in the Holy Land developed quickly and some of the ideas may have helped to improve castles in Europe.

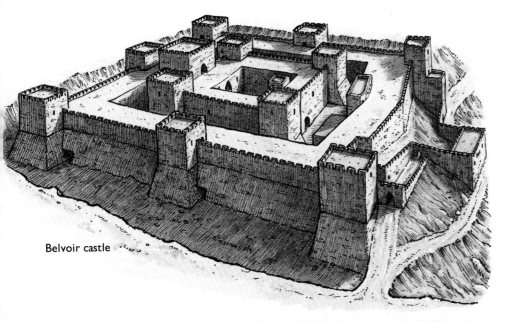

Belvoir castle

Beaumaris castle

Source I
The Cost of Crusading

i   Everyone is to give one-tenth of his income and property in this year as a tax for the land of Jerusalem. If anyone gives less than he ought by the assessment of the collectors, four or six true men from the parish should be chosen to swear under oath how much should have been paid. Priests and knights who have taken the cross will not pay this tithe.

(Roger of Howden, an English chronicler, recording the tax collected throughout England and France in 1188 to pay for the crusade to recapture Jerusalem. It became known as the Saladin Tithe or tenth)

ii Household costs	£
Food	31,595
Clothes and furs for the king	104
Mantles for knights and priests	312
Arrows and clothes for knights and priests	12,910
Gifts of robes and silver	771
Alms (gifts to the poor and needy)	1,515
Crossbowmen and sergeants	4,494
115 horses and mules	1,916
Total household costs of the king and queen	**53,617**
War and shipping	
Wages for knights	57,093
Gifts and payments to knights serving without wages	23,253
Mounted crossbowmen and sergeants	22,242
264 war horses	6,789
Foot crossbowmen and sergeants	29,575
Carpenters, war-engineers and labourers	689
General costs	66,793
Shipping	5,729
Total	**212,159**

(Extracts from the accounts of Louis IX of France for 1252, recording the costs of his expedition to the Holy Land)

Source J

i   The pilgrims rose in cruelty against the Jews who were scattered throughout the cities of the Rhineland. They inflicted a most cruel slaughter on them, especially in the kingdom of Lorraine, claiming that this was the beginning of their pilgrimage and the killing would be of service against the enemies of Christianity.

(Albert of Aachen, a German chronicler, describing the slaughter of Jews at the beginning of the People's Crusade of 1096. Crusaders wanted revenge for the loss of Jerusalem. They blamed the Jews for the Crucifixion of Christ and attacked them because they were easy, and sometimes rich, targets)

ii   Throughout England, many of those preparing to join the Crusade to Jerusalem decided they would first rise up against the Jews before they attacked the Moslems. On 6 February 1190 in Norwich all the Jews found in their homes were slaughtered. On 7 March many were killed at Stamford during the fair. At York about fifty were killed.

(Ralph of Diceto, an English chronicler, describing reactions in England at the beginning of the Third Crusade. Jews were also attacked and killed in London and other towns)

Source K

Cotton	Orange	Saffron
Spinach	Sherbert	Sugar
Syrup	Lemon	Caravan

These are all words that Europeans borrowed from Arabic. The Crusaders brought back some of these words but there was always trade between Christians and Moslems which added new words to each other's languages. The word most connected with the Crusades is Assassin. The Hashishiyun or Assassins were a group of secret murderers. People believed they were drugged with hashish by their master, the Old Man of the Mountains, before setting out. These assassins could be hired to kill leaders on both sides but their real targets were their religious enemies. Their ideas about Islam made them enemies of other groups of Moslems.

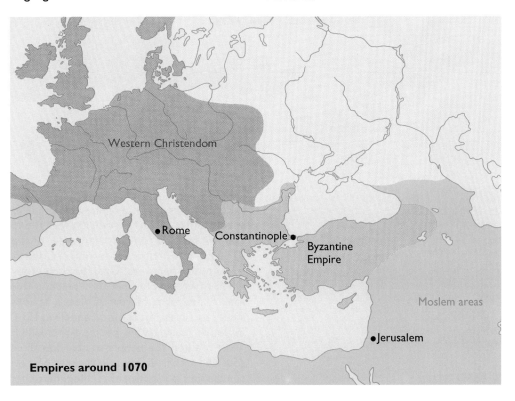

Empires around 1070

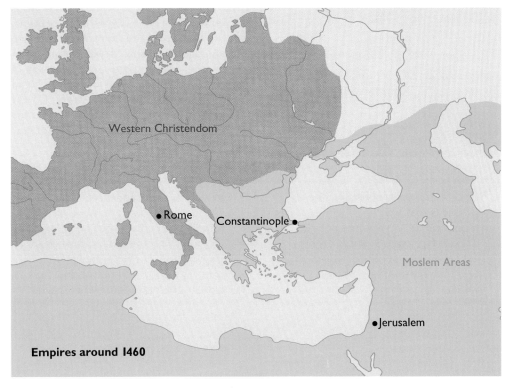

Empires around 1460

Source L

In 1070 the Eastern Christian (Byzantine) Empire was under attack by Moslem forces but was still very large. Unfortunately, the western Crusaders never allied successfully with the eastern emperors in Constantinople. Slowly the Eastern Empire grew weaker until, in 1453, Constantinople was captured by the Moslems.

Source M

Moslem forces used carrier pigeons to send messages, although they were not always successful. Messages that were too long and heavy caused the birds to crashland. In 1124 a pigeon was sent to the Moslem forces defending Tyre, telling them that reinforcements were on the way. However, the bird landed in the Crusaders' camp and its message was changed to say that no help was coming. The Moslem defenders surrendered! However, pigeon post was so useful that the Crusaders used it too and took the idea back to Europe.

Source N

Many Christians still live today in the Middle East. Unfortunately, some still live in conflict with their neighbours. This is most clear in the Lebanon where the country is divided between Christians and different Moslem groups. The Christians, known as Maronite Christians, are fiercely independent and look back to the 1100's as their greatest days. Then they were part of the larger Christian kingdom of Jerusalem. The Moslem groups still follow the idea of 'Jihad', or holy war, which Saladin pursued against the Crusaders.

Source P

Members of the St. John Ambulance Brigade, distant descendants of the Hospitallers, the Knights of the Hospital of St. John of Jerusalem

Source O

When explorers and adventurers sailed to America they took their religion with them. They wanted to convert the people of the Americas to Christianity – a kind of Crusade to help non-believers. Unfortunately, they killed more people than they helped. This source describes Hernan Cortes's actions after a battle against the local people in 1519, in which many native people were killed: 'Cortes asked the people to abandon their gods and sacrifices. He told them as best he could about our holy faith, telling them that we were Christians and worshipped one true God. He then showed them a most sacred image of our Lady with her precious son in her arms and told them that we worshipped it because it was the image of the mother of our Lord God, who was in heaven. The Indians asked for it to be given to them to keep in their town. Cortes agreed and told them to build a fine altar for it. Next morning he ordered two of our carpenters to make a very tall cross.'

CAUSES AND CONSEQUENCES: EFFECTS OF THE CRUSADES

1   Choose one consequence of the Crusades that was
    a political b social c religious
2   Choose two consequences of the Crusades that were short-term and two that were long-term.

3   Which two consequences of the Crusades do you think were most important? Explain your choices.
4   Do you think the Crusades were an important event? Use the list on page 43 to help you decide and then explain the reasons for your answer.

🕮 Understanding other people

By investigating the Crusades you have learned more about how we study history, why people have different views about events and whether the Crusades themselves were important. The final reason for studying the Crusades – or any other event in history – is that it teaches us more about people.

Think about the people who went on Crusades. Many travelled thousands of miles from their homes in ships we would not dare go in. They did not know how long they would be away or whether they would ever see their families and friends again. What were those people like?

In some ways they were different from us. Their clothes, transport, the way they spoke and the houses they lived in were all different. More importantly, their religion was so important to them that they risked their lives as pilgrims and Crusaders. Today many people find it difficult to understand how important religion was to people in the past.

However, people in the past were just like us in other ways. They loved their families, enjoyed their food, played games, laughed and cried, felt lonely and excited, just like we do. They were like us in another way too. They did not understand other people very well.

Many Crusaders did not realise that Jerusalem was a holy city for Moslems as well as for Christians. They thought they were right and the others were wrong, when really there was bravery and good, cruelty and evil on both sides, not just one.

These problems still happen today. If you want to understand why conflicts, wars or arguments continue nowadays, you need to think about the people involved in the same way that you have

thought about the people at the time of the Crusades. Do the people today understand each others' ideas and beliefs? Do they think about the real people on the other side or do they only think about the 'enemy'? Have they stopped trying to understand altogether? Perhaps the history of the past is worth studying because it helps us to understand the people of today?

Thousands and thousands died in battle, fighting for their religion. Does the use of the word 'Crusades' instead of 'wars' make these events seem more glorious and less cruel than they really were?

A scene from a manuscript describing the First Crusade. More Crusaders died from disease than in war. Many also died on the long and dangerous journey to the Holy Land. Going on Crusade was a hard and difficult experience.

Three religions united – Christians, Moslems and Jews, sitting in Abraham's lap. This illustration is from a twelfth century manuscript. Do you think many people believed that the different religions would be united in heaven?

Index

Acre   27–28
Arsuf   29
Assassins   45

Children's Crusade   36, 38
Christian Attitudes   9, 16–18
Chronicles and Chroniclers
    Christian:
    Fulcher of Chartres   9, 17
    Gerald of Wales   39
    Journey of King Richard   18, 21, 27, 29, 31, 42
    Radulph of Caen   14, 18
    Roger of Howden   26, 44
    William of Tyre   9, 17, 21, 24, 32–33, 41
    Moslem:
    Baha ad-Din   21, 26, 31, 36, 42
    Ibn al-Athir   5, 13, 14, 21, 23, 24, 42
    Ibn Jubayr   9, 14
    Ibn al Qalinisi   13
    Imad ad-Din   14, 24
    Usamah Ibn Munqidh   10–11, 13–14, 17, 21, 22
Constantinople   43, 45
Crusade:
    First   3, 5, 6, 47
    Second   6
    Third   5, 6, 20–33, 41
    Fourth   6, 43
Crusader Castles   7, 13, 44
Crusades after 1204   6, 35
Crusades in Europe   35

Dome of the Rock   5

Edward I, King of England   38–39
Effects of the Crusades   43–46

Frederick Barbarossa   26–27

Godfrey of Bouillon, King of Jerusalem   5
Greek Fire   28
Guy, King of Jerusalem   22–24, 28

Hattin, Battle of   20, 22–24
Henry IV, King of England   38
Henry VIII, King of England   35, 38
Holy Sepulchre   5

Islam, Five Pillars of   14

Jerusalem   4–5, 12, 18, 25, 29–30, 32–33, 41, 47

Knights Templar and Hospitaller   11, 24, 46

Louis IX, King of France   38, 44

Medicine   9, 13, 17
Moslem Attitudes   10–15
Muhammad   5, 12, 14

Nur ad-Din   14, 20

People's Crusade   4, 36
Peter the Hermit   4, 36
Philip, King of France   26–29

Richard the Lionheart, King of England   26–33
Routes to the Holy Land   4, 27

Saladin   5, 20–25, 27, 29–31, 42
Saladin Tithe   44
Soldiers and Weapons   6, 17, 23, 28–29, 32

Urban II   3

Women Crusaders   36

Zangi, Imad al-Din   13–14, 20

⟪ Acknowledgements

The publishers would like to thank the following for permission to reproduce photographs:

Aerofilms p7, p44; Ancient Art and Architecture p11, p26, p31 (bottom), p36 (bottom); Bibliotheque Nationale p12, p17 (bottom) p24, p28 (bottom), p33, p47 (middle); British Library p15, p16 (bottom), p17 (middle), p18, p21 (top), p31 (top) p36 (top), p36 (middle), p37, p38, p42; Burghersbibliotek, Berne p47 (top); Conway Library, Cortauld Institute p4; Corpus Christi College, Cambridge p16 ([top), p23, p30; Edinburgh University Library p17 (top); Giraudon p47 (bottom); Index, Florence p46 (top); Magnum p46 (middle); Mansell p21 (bottom); MAS p9, p28; Order of St John p43; St John's p46 (bottom); Sonia Halliday p5 (bottom), p5 (top), p25, p32, p41

Cover photograph: Ancient Art and Architecture

Illustrations: Martin Cottam

Maps: Technical Graphics (OUP)